# THE GREAT RACE

# The Great Race

*Britain to Australia 1919*

COLIN HOLCOMBE

Colin Holcombe

Acknowledgements

In researching material for this book I am grateful to :

The State Library of South Australia

Sea Land and Air published by The Wireless Press 1919

Bristol Aerospace Museum


ISBN : 978-1-5272-8967-3

First Printing, 2021

# Contents

# Chapter 1

# Background

In 1919, only sixteen years after the Wright brothers and the birth of powered flight four miles south of Kitty Hawk, North Carolina, aviation was no longer in its infancy. The horrors of The First World War had seen it through puberty and in adolescence, it was now seeking to find a role for itself in the world. Was it to remain just a military asset, a platform from which to view or strike at an enemy, or a toy of the rich adventurere with which to entertain the public with pleasure flights and daring aerial displays? Or could it be more than that, much more. Was it possible that aviation could open the world up to international travel on a scale never imagined? Well of course we now know that aviation has done many of those things. It has enabled international cooperation between nations to fly much needed aid to areas of national disater, and made travel between countries easier for the general public, making different populations more aware of each other, and hopefully more tolerant, of other cultures.

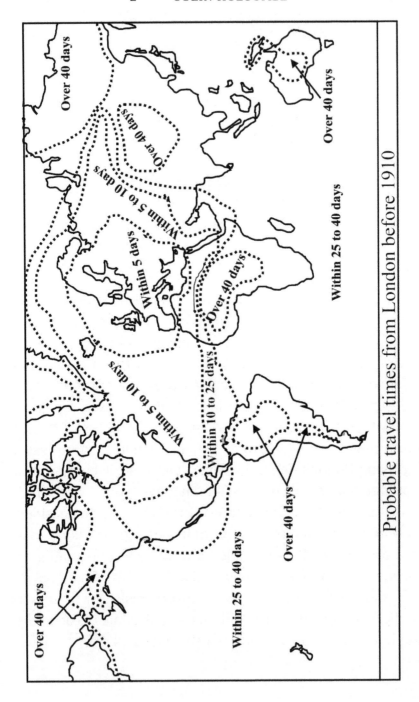

Probable travel times from London before 1910

Unfortunately of course, as seems to be the case with most scientific or technological advances, it has also provided governments and armies with a much better "weapons platform" enabling them to strike at enemies from vast distances, delivering what the military proudly describe as "Global Reach".

What the world of aviation was looking to do in 1919, was to develop air routes between countries that would stop international travel from having to be measured in weeks and months and instead have it measured in hours and days. Louis Charles Blériot had crossed the English Channel on the 25th July 1909, winning the Daily Mail prize of £1,000. It was an important landmark in aviation history, but such landmarks were being established at quite a rate back then. Pilots were flying their machines higher, faster and for longer on what must have seemed a monthly basis.

The Great War of 1914-1918, the war that was to end all wars, meant that advances in aeroplane design and technology were coming thick and fast. Aircraft were now being flown every day in all but the very worst weather conditions. Taking off and landing, often from unsuitable surfaces, and being pushed to their operational limits in aerial combat, so they had to be constantly serviced and maintained. Improvements came quickly, not just in the form of advances in aerodynamics and types of construction, but in avionics and engine design as well. Huge advances were made in both engine design and manufacture as well, making them not only more powerful but much more reliable. Simple changes, such as providing an inline engine with an overhead camshaft, allowing the propeller to be fitted higher, which gave greater ground clearance and therefore allowed shorter, more robust landing gear.

The early inline, "pusher engines" of the first aircraft, that had the propeller situated behind the engine and literally pushed the aircraft through the air, had rapidly given way to what we would now regard as the more normal "tracker engine", that is situated in front of the power source, and pulls the aircraft through the air.

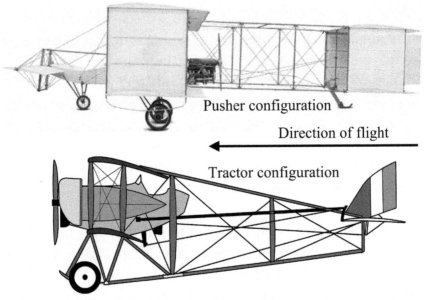

Voicin Biplane with pusher configuration and G 9 with tractor configuration

Even before the end of the war engines like the Gnome Omega, the first practical rotary engine, were taking over from the inline engine and throughout the war the radial and rotary engines saw dominance, although towards the end, inline engine was begining to make it's comeback, with engines like the water-cooled twelve-cylinder inline Liberty 12-A built by Dayton-Wright in America.

A Gnome 7 cylinder rotary engine

The difference between a Radial and Rotory engine is simply that a radial engine has the cylinders arranged around the camshaft and the propeller rotates with the shaft. In a rotary engine, the camshaft is attached to the airframe and the engine block and cylinders rotate around it, the propeller being bolted to the face of the engine block.

The period between the two world wars obviously saw a drop in the demand for military aircraft. Nobody suspected that the world would be fighting again so soon after such carnage, but this in no way meant that interest in aviation diminished.

In fact, interest was growing, and now turned towards the civil use of aircraft. The general public were taking a keen interest in all things aviation.

Lots of military aircraft were sold off to civilians after the war and flying schools were being established all over. In America, farmers were paying private pilots to dust their crops for them. It was the age of wing-walking and the flying circus. The public were being offered pleasure flights and the first air-mail and passenger services were beginning to be established by 1919. In fact, 1919 was to prove a momentous year in the history of aviation.

The Liberty 12-A

During the 14th and 15th of June 1919 the British aviators, John Alcock and Arthur Brown, made the first non-stop flight across the Atlantic in a Vickers Vimy twin engine converted bomber.

Alcock and Brown's Vickers Vimy, powered by two Rolls Royce Eagle 360 hp engines and carrying 865 imperial gallons of fuel, took off from Lester's Field, in St. John's, Newfoundland.

During the flight at around 17:20, the wind-driven electrical generator on the aircraft failed, depriving the intrepid duo of radio contact, as well as their intercom and more crucially, their heating. As if that wasn't enough, an exhaust pipe burst shortly afterwards, causing a loud noise which subsequently made conversation between the two airmen practically impossible.

Later, they had to fly through a thick bank of fog that prevented Brown from using his sextant to navigate. Blind flying in fog or cloud should only ever be undertaken with gyroscopic instruments, which they didn't have, and Alcock twice became disoriented, lost control of the aircraft and nearly crashed into the sea after a spiral dive. He also had to deal with a broken trim control which caused the plane to become increasingly nose-heavy as fuel was consumed.

At a little after midnight, Brown managed to get a brief glimpse of the stars and was able to fleetingly use his sextant, and thankfully verify that they were miraculously still on course. Then, at 3:00 a.m. they flew into a large snowstorm and their instruments iced up. The plane itself was also in danger of icing and becoming unflyable, a truly perilous turn of events.

Eventually however, due to a combination of skill, dogged determination and good luck, they made landfall at 8:15 on 15th June 1919, not far from their intended landing place, in Clifden, County Galway, after a slightly less than sixteen-hour flight.

The aircraft was damaged on finally setting down because they had landed on what appeared, from the air, to be a suitable green field, but which in fact turned out to be Derrygilmlagh Bog, and this caused the aircraft to nose-over on landing. Thankfully neither of the brave airmen were hurt. Brown later said that if the weather had been kinder to them, they could have pressed on to London.

The Secretary of State for Air, Winston Churchill, presented Alcock and Brown with the Daily Mail prize for the first crossing of the Atlantic Ocean in less than 72 consecutive hours. They had carried a small amount of mail on the flight making it also the first transatlantic airmail flight.

The two aviators were awarded the honour of Knight Commander of the Most Excellent Order of the British Empire (KBE) by King George V at Windsor Castle, one week later.

So, now that such a large expanse of water had been crossed, what was to be the next step in establishing the much needed international air routes?

Well, the Australian Government knew what they thought should be the next big achievement after all, they must have been feeling a little cut off down there at the bottom of the world, far away from the northern hemisphere where aerodromes were being built and airlines established.

Australia had always placed great importance on aviation for the transportation of goods and mail, so, on the 19th March 1919, the Commonwealth Government of Australia offered a prize of £10,000 for the first flight from Great Britain to Australia, under specific conditions.

The initial announcement was made by the then Acting Prime Minister W. A. Watt, who stated that the proposal had been communicated to the British Air Ministry by the Prime Minister, Hon. W.M. Hughes, some weeks previously and had been commended by the authorities in England.

The following evening, March 20<sup>th</sup> a banquet was held at the Savoy Hotel under the auspices of the Society of British Aircraft Constructors

The Chairman of the Society. Mr. H. White Smith, C. B. E., (who was also chairman and a director of the British and Colonial Aeroplane Co. Ltd. Bristol,) proposed the toast of "The Royal Air Force," which was responded to by Right Hon. W. S. Churchill, Colonel T. J. C. Moore-Brabazon, M.P. Major-General the Right Hon. J. E. B. Seely, C. G., C. M. B., D. S. O., and Major-General Sir P. H. Sykes, K. C. B., C. M. G. (former Chief of Air Staff, and now Controller of Civil Aviation in Great Britain).

From the press response however, it would seem that not everybody viewed the proposal favourably, as the Argus (Melbourne), declared that the achievement, *"Would be a commonplace in aviation, and that there was no necessity to throw away thousands of pounds on the project."*

The Age (Melbourne), in a leading article, described it as *"a circus flight...a poorly disguised attempt at self-advertisement at the expense of the Australian public"* and predicted that the person who pays would cling to the hope that the prize would not be claimed before Parliament reassembled, when the Ministry could be forced to reject its offer.

Punch (Melbourne), remarked that *"We seem to have plenty of money in this country"*

The New York Times asserted that *"Christopher Columbus did not take one-tenth the risks that these air pioneers will face. They will be throwing dice with death."*

The Corowa Free Press (New South Wales) inquired, *"How many people care whether there is an aerial mail service be-*

*tween Great Britain and Australia or not?"* and added *"They ought to carry as passengers on the experimental voyage as many Federal Members as possible...and leave them somewhere else!"*

Despite the controversy, plans went ahead. Each flight was to take place under the competition rules of the Royal Aero Club, that would supervise the start, and control the competition generally.

It was stated that "although between 12,000 and 14,000 miles of land and sea have to be covered, the task, while it imposes a great strain upon the machines, does not present anything like the risks of the Transatlantic flight. The route is by way of Alexandria and Singapore, at which places the competitors have to report for the identification of their machines. The airmen will presumably follow the course already successfully accomplished by R.A.F. Handley Page machines as far as India - across France, down the Mediterranean to Alexandria, thence to Baghdad, and on to Singapore. From Singapore to Australia the route will lie across the islands of the Malay Archipelago. The oversea flight will nowhere exceed a few hundred miles.

Brigadier-General A. E. Borton, D.S.O. A. F. C (RAF) and Captain Ross Macpherson Smith, M.C., D.F.C., a South Australian pilot, who was the first man to pilot a machine from Egypt to India, are already preparing landing-places between Singapore and Australia. His attempt will, however, be independent of the Commonwealth prize."

Brigadier-General Borton reported on the 19th September that between Calcutta and the Dutch East Indies the only landing grounds suitable for immediate use were the racecourses at Rangoon (Burma) and Singapore. Beyond Singapore, where the route lies over the Dutch Islands, the next place at which good landing facilities existed was Bandong (Java), and thence no landing ground was (then) available on the intervening 1760 miles to Darwin.

In May 1919, Billy Hughes, Prime Minister of Australia and Senator George Pearce, Minister for Defence (Australia), in consultation with The Royal Aero Club, stated that valid aircrews must all be Australian nationals, and the aircraft must have been constructed in the British Empire.

## The Rules and Regulations

1: The Australian Government has offered the sum of £10,000 to be awarded to the first pilot who shall accomplish the flight in an aeroplane or seaplane from Great Britain to Australia within 720 consecutive hours (30 days).

2: The offer will remain open until midnight on the 31$^{st}$ December 1920 by which date the flight must have been completed.

3: The complete aircraft and all its component parts must have been entirely constructed within the confines of the British Empire. Raw materials may be obtained from other countries.

4: The pilots and all the crew must be of Australian nationality in accordance with the laws of the Australian Commonwealth.

5: Entries are to be made to the Royal Aero Club, 3 Clifford Street, London W. 1. The entry form, which must be accompanied by the entry fee of £100, must be sent to the secretary of the club at least seven days before the start is made. All entry fees received will be applied towards payment of the expenses of the Royal Aero Club in conducting the competition. Any balance not so expended will be refunded, prorate, to the entrants.

6: Identification of aircraft: Only one aircraft may be used throughout the flight. Incidental replacement and repairs to the aircraft and motors may be made en route, but neither may be changed as a whole. In the case of a seaplane, it may be taken ashore for such repars and replacements. Five parts of the aircraft and five parts of each motor will be stamped or otherwise marked, and at least two marked parts of each of these five must be in place at the control and at the finishing point.

7: Starting Place: The start must be made from Hounslow Aerodrome or Calshot Seaplane Station. All starts must be made under the supervision of an official or officials appointed by the Royal Aero Club.

8: Finishing Place: The point at which the competitors must finish in Australia will be in the neighbourhood of Port Darwin, and will be announced later.

9: Control: A control station will be established on the route of the flight at Singapore. Competitors must alight at this Control for the purposes of identification.

10: Towing: Towing on the water is not prohibited, but the total distance of such towing must not exceed100 miles, of which not more than 50 miles shall be consecutive.

11: Timing: The time of starting will be the time the aircraft leaves the ground or water, and the time of arrival will be deemed to be the time of crossing the coast-line in the neighbourhood of Port Darwin.

## General

1: A competitor, by entering, thereby agrees that he is bound by the regulations herein contained, or to be hereafter issued in connection with this competition.

2: The interpretation of these regulations, or of any to be hereafter issued shall rest entirely with the Royal Aero Club.

3: The competitor shall be solely responsible to the officials for the due observance of these regulations, and shall be the person with whom the officials will deal in respect thereof, or of any questions arising out of this competition.

4: A competitor, by entering, waives any right of action against the Royal Aero Club or the Australian Government for any damages sustained by him in consequence of any act or omission on the part of the officials of the Royal Aero Club or the Australian Government or their representatives or servants or any fellow competitor.

5: The aircraft shall at all times be at the risk in all respects of the competitor, who shall be deemed by entry to agree to waive all claim for injury either to himself, or his passengers or his aircraft, or his employees, or workmen and to assume all liability for damage to third parties or their property, and to indemnify the Royal Aero Club and the Australian Government in respect thereof.

6: The Committee of the Royal Aero Club reserves to itself the right, with the consent of the Australian Government, to add to, amend, or omit any of these rules should it think fit.

On the 21$^{st}$ August the Royal Aero Club announced the following supplementary regulations.

1: No start will be permitted until subsequent to 8$^{th}$ September 1919.

2: Machines must have a flying range of at least 500 miles.

3: A Competent navigator must be carried, who may be the pilot.

4: Competitors must satisfy the Royal Aero Club that landing places are available.

5: At the request of the Australian Government, it has been decided that the motor or motors may be changed en route.

## Six teams finally competed.

Captain Ross Macpherson Smith with his brother Keith Macpherson Smith as co-pilot and mechanics, Sergeant W. H. (Wally) Shiers and J. M. (Jim) Bennett, in a Vickers Vimy.

Captain George Campbell Matthews AFC as pilot, and Sergeant Thomas D. Kay as mechanic, in a Sopwith Wallaby

Lieutenant Roger M. Douglas, M.C. D.C.M. and Lieutenant J.S.L. Ross, in an Alliance P.2. Seabird.

Lieutenant V. Rendle, Captain G. H. Wilkins, Lieutenant D.R. Williams, and Lieutenant Garnsey St. C. Potts as crew and flying a Blackburn Kangaroo. They had originally selected an Australian Charles Kingford Smith to be their navigator but Smith withdrew from the contest and Captain Hurbert Wilkins MC took his place.

Captain Cedric E. Howell and Lieutenant George Henry Fraser, left London in a Martinsyde Type A Mk. 1 (G-EAMR) aircraft.

Lieutenant Ray Parer with co-pilot Lieutenant John C. McIntosh, flying an Airco DH 9.

There were also two other entries, one from two Frenchmen. A pilot, Etienne M. Poulet and his mechanic, Jean Benoit. These men would not be entitled to win the prize, even if they arrived first, as they did not fit the criteria to be eligible to enter the contest. They were not Australian for a start, and they intended to fly in a French built Caudron G4 biplane and depart from Paris. But. despite not being eligible to win the prize money, Poulet and Benoit were determined to be the first to fly from Europe to Australia.

There was also an entry from Lieutenant Bert Hinckler, D. S. M. of Bundaberg, Queensland who had worked his passage to England in order to enlist in the Royal Naval Air Service as soon as the war started in 1914.

Hinckler intended to fly alone in a Sopwith Dove biplane fitted with a Le Rhone engine, and spent almost two months planning for the race, including flying non-stop from Brooklands to Edinburgh.

Bert Hinckler

Lieutenant Hinckler later withdrew from the competition. It was annouced in Australia that this was due to his machine having insufficient flying range to comply with supplementary regulations announced by the Aero Club on August 21$^{st}$. This however, was far from the truth, as the regulations stated that aircraft must have a range of at least 500 miles and Hinckler had already planned one leg of 1,000 miles. The real stumbling block was his decision to fly solo.

Just how well Lieutenant Hinckler would have done, had he been allowed to fly solo, we shall never know. However we do know that he went on to be recongnised as one of Australia's greatest long distance fliers. His solo flight from England to Australia in 1928 was chosen as the most outstanding aviation achievement of the year by both the Royal Aero Club and the Federation Aeronautique Internationle.

He was killed tragically on the 7th January 1933 when the Puss Moth he was flying crashed in the Italian Apennines.

# Chapter 2

# Preparations

Although the invention of the aeroplane had greatly increased the expectation of how fast one could travel from place to place, there were still limitations and international travel was still largely measured in terms of days rather than hours. One of the biggest obstacles in the early days of air travel, apart from the unreliability of engines, was the lack of suitable aerodromes and airfields.

Immediately after the Armistice, an air service was set up between London and Paris, for the purpose of accelerating communication with the Peace Conference, and a London to Paris ,and London to Brussels air service set up by the Air Transport and Travel Company. Messrs Handley Page were the first of many commercial lines set up after the war, radiating from London to the commercial centres of Europe.

The British Empire, with bases in Britain, Canada, India, Newfoundland, Egypt, South Africa, and New Zealand as well as Australia, was uniquely placed to set up international air routes.

Between the winter of 1918 and the spring of 1919 an international Air Convention was established and agreement was reached on the establishment of an International Committee for Air Navigation. The Convention, which was signed by all the Allies except for the United States, Japan and Canada, allowed aircraft of one contracted State freedom of innocent passage over the territory of another. It forbid the flight of an aircraft of a non-contracted State over the territory of a contracted State, and laid down detailed regulations based upon those already adopted in Britain. Certain neutrals such as Holland, Switzerland and the Scandinavian countries were still considering whether or not to draw up similar agreements.

The First World War had seen a huge increase in available landing sites in Europe and Asia and the R.A.F. had carried out flights from Cairo to India looking for a suitable air route. Towards the end of the war in 1918, Brigadier-General A. E. Borton had flown from England to Palestine in a Handley-Page bomber with Ross Smith as pilot, and the success of this flight prompted him to plan a further flight from Palestine to Baghdad accompanied by Major-General W.G.H. Salmond KCMG, CB, DSO, with Captain Ross Smith as pilot and Sergeants J.M. Bennett and Sergeant W.H. Shiers as mechanics, after which they pioneered a route to India, arriving in Calcutta on 10th December 1918.

This was the longest flight that had ever been made at that time.

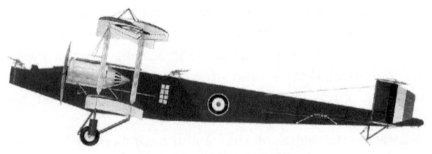

Drawing of a Handley-Page 0/400 Bomber

Although there were a number of suitable landing and re-fuelling sites between Britain and India when the competition was announced, the rest of the route needed to be surveyed and landing grounds established.

Coincidentally, General Borton had been granted permission by the British Air Ministry to charter a ship so that he could survey the route from India to Australia. The Air Ministry acceded to the request and Captain Ross Smith agreed to accompany him on the trip as Staff-Captain.

Brigadier General Amyas Borton

On the 10th February 1919 an Indian Government ship, R.I.M.S. Sphinx, was made available and sailed from Calcutta with Borton and Ross on board, together with 7,000 gallons of petrol that was to be distributed at selected points along the route.

Things started reasonably well, but shortly after leaving the port of Chittagong, two days out of Calcutta a fire broke out on board ship and dispite all efforts to save the ship, she had to be abandoned and the Sphinx exploded. It was a miracle that both General Borton and Ross escaped with their lives, however the ship itself was utterly destroyed.

It was only after some lengthy negotiation that the Indian Government finally agreed to supply another ship, the R.I.M.S. Minto, but this was only on condition that no petrol was carried.

They had planned to travel all the way to Darwin but although the survey was considered successful, having called in at Burma, Malaysia, Singapore, Indonesia and Thailand over a three-month period, both men suffered bouts of malaria that caused them to leave the Minto after being treated by a Dutch doctor at Koepang.

On their return to Calcutta, they discovered that the Handley-Page aircraft which they had planned to fly to Australia had crashed in the north-west frontier during a storm. It was also then that they heard of the Australian Government's offer of a £10,000 prize for the first flight from Britain to Australia.

At a conference in London on the 19th September 1919 attended by members of the Royal Aero Club, the Australian Government and the Air Ministry, General Borton reported on the results of his survey from Calcutta to Timor, stating that the only suitable landing sites between India and Indonesia were racecourses at Rangoon and Singapore. He also emphasised that the racecourses would need prior warning of any aircrafts arrival so that hurdles and other obstacles could be removed in time.

What is unclear however, is why in his report, General Borton failed to mention that the headquarters of the Siamese Flying Corps was located at Don Muang, Bangkok, where there was not only an airfield but also several aircraft hangers and a fully equipped up-to-date workshop.

It would seem that Thailand, with its thick expanses of jungle, was quick to foresee the importance of air travel and had introduced an airmail route as early as February 1919 with its very own postmark.

General Borton went on to tell the conference that after Singapore the only landing ground before Darwin was at Bandoeng in what was then the Dutch East Indies and still some 1,700 miles from the final destination.

It is clear that General Borton was very keen to be a part of a team himself, but not being an Australian, he was debarred from entering. Instead he approched Vickers Ltd on behalf of Ross and requested they supply him with a machine for the flight.

Bankok to Chandaburi airmails dated 1920s

Four days before the London Conference the Australian Aero Club had appointed a sub-committee consisting of Reginald Lloyd, Sydney H. Deamer, Edward J. Hart and Captain Geoffrey F. Hughs, to gather information and make recommendations as to what action was to be taken by the club.

Reginald Lloyd had in fact announced his plan for an air service between London and Sydney as far back as October 1918. He asserted that using a Handley-Page aircraft, the distance could be covered in 150 hours with each leg of the journey being in the region of 300 miles but, despite having formed a company, "Aerial Services Limited" with Sir Edmund Barton of Sydney, nothing had come of it.

The sub-committee approached the Australian Government with a list of questions, to which they received the following answers:

Question:  What are the conditions of the flight?

Answer:  Rules and Regulations to be prepared by the Royal Aero Club.

Question:  Are entrants able to start before the given date?

Answer:  No.

Question:  What is the start date?

Answer:  8$^{th}$ September 1919.

Question:  Will the flight be confined to a specific route?

Answer:  A specific route has been laid down but it may not always be adhered to.

Question:  What provision, if any, have been made for landing stations along the route and where are they located?

Answer:  The provision of landing stations between Great Britain and India has already been undertaken. Concerning landing grounds between India and Australia, the Prime Minister has received from the Minister of Defence the following communication dated 22$^{nd}$ September 1919, a copy of which was forwarded on the 2$^{nd}$ October by the Secretary, Department of Defence, to the Honorary Secretary, Australian Aero Club New South Wales Section. *"The only landing grounds now available past India are: Rangoon, Bangkok, Singapore and Bandoeng."*

Question: What provisions, if any, have been made for the assistance of pilots who may require same, particularly in Australia?

Answer: Two of our flying officers, Lieutenants McGinness and Fysh, have travelled by car from Cloncurry, via Burketown and Booraloola, to Katherine River, and report the route quite unsuitable and dangerous for flying. They are now getting landing grounds ready at Darwin, Katherine, Avon Downs Station and Cloncurry. The route to Membourne, thence via Longgrech, Chaleville, Narromine, Cootamundra and Albany has been mapped. This should be sufficient for machines that can reach Australia, but local machines travelling the same route can get petrol at any inland town.

Question: Which is the terminal point of the flight?

Answer: Terminal point of route is Darwin.

Question: What arrangements have been made for the establishment of control centres and the appointment of officials?

Answer: An official of the Royal Aero Club is stationed at the Singapore control. Between Singapore and Darwin there are no officials. With reference to appointment of officials between Darwin and Melbourne, a statement was made by Sir Joseph Cook, Minister for the Navy, on the 24t October1919, as follows.

*"The Australian Navy ship (H.M.S. Brisbane) will co-operate by maintaining a patrol at sea beteen Koepang, on the island of Timor, and Darwin. Stocks of petrol will be made available at Darwin, Cloncurry, Charleville and Narromine. At these places there will be a flying officer with instructions for the guidance of competitors, and to assist generally. Arrangements for the flight prior to reaching Australia are in the hands of the Air Ministry and the Royal Aero Club of England."*

Question:    Will any entrant be permitted to attempt the flight once the authorities have satisfied themselves that arrangement have been completed for the prevention of disaster from avoidable causes?

Answer:    This can be answered by referring the Rules and Regulations.

George Foster Pearce

In London Senator George Pearce, the Australian Minister of Defence, had cabled home to Australia declaring that international flying was now possible over France, Italy and Greece and that the Netherlands Embassy was taking action to issue landing permits for Holland and the Dutch East Indies. He had also requested the authorities in Rangoon and Singapore to remove any hurdles or other obstruction to landing from their racecourses between the last week in October and the first two weeks in November. This would have meant postponement of races, and would not have gone down well with the authorities especially, as it turned out, as the first aircraft didn't actually arrive in Rangoon until 30th November.

The Australian Aero Club sub-committee made the following recommendations and observations.

## Recommendations:

1: That a proper landing ground be provided at Darwin.

2: That suitable hanger accommodation be arranged along with adequate staff of efficient air mechanics.

3: That means be provided whereby assistance, food and other necessities could reach competitors requiring same.

4: That the Department of Defence provide one or more aeroplanes from Point Cook to be stationed at Darwin and that from the time the competitors expected to arrive, these aeroplanes shall patrol the coast daily within reasonable distance of Darwin, keeping a lookout for competitors who may be in difficulties through forced landings.

5: That these aeroplanes shall carry supplies of food and water which could be dropped to distressed airmen by means of parachutes.

## Observations:

The sub-committee also made the following observations:

That a flight from Britain to Australia by a single machine should not under present conditions be regarded as an indication of the commercial possibilities of aviation.

They further stated that, although there is no single stage of the proposed route that could not be flown by existing machines if ordinary aerodrome facilities were provided, and that the flight could be accomplished by relays of machines if such aerodromes were properly equipped along the route, the competitors in the present attempt are exposed to grave risk, due to the lack of landing stations.

# Chapter 3

# The Caudron G4 Team

*The Team.*

*Etienne Poulet and Jean Benoist*

Very litttle seems to be known about Jean Benoist other than that he was the mechanic chosen by Poulet for the attempt to be the first to fly to Australia from Europe.

Etienne Poulet was born in 1890, in Lommes, in the north of France, on 10<sup>th</sup> June 1890. He studied at the Industrial School of Electricity in Paris, before joining the French Military Air Force College, and it was while he was studying there that he obtained his civilian pilot certificate number 709 in January 1912 flying a Caudron aircraft, a machine that he was to become very familiar with.

Between being released from military service in 1913, when he joined the Caudron aeroplane company as a test pilot, and 1919, he became a well-known and much praised French aviator, alongside Himelman and Roland Garros. He demonstrated the Caudron aircraft in aerobatic displays in France, Germany, Switzerland and Austria and was one of the first pilots to perform loop the loop.

Etienne Poulet (left) and Jean Benoist

With the outbreak of hostilities in 1914 he was mobilised and posted to General Headquarters as a member of C.11. Squadron. He was soon attached once again to the Caudron factory where he test flew an amazing 1,400 aircraft during the war period.

A good friend of Poulet's and fellow aviator Jules Védrines, had planned a tour of the world in five parts, one part of which was to be a flight from Paris to Melbourne.

Employed at the Gnome engine factory, he had already acquired some notoriety, having been the first person to fly over Paris and winning both the Paris to Madrid air race and the Gordon Bennett Cup.

However before the details of his world flight were announced he was tragically killed in a crash on the 21st April 1919, when attempting to fly a Caudron C.23 from Villacoublay to Rome, Italy. After an engine failed he attempted a forced landing, but crashed near St. Rambert d'Albon near Lyon, killing himself and his mechanic, Marcel Guillain.

Saddened by his friend's tragic death, Poulet announced his plans to be the first to fly from Europe to Australia and intended to give the earnings from any displays and exhibitions to the Védrines family, a widow and four children. When the prize of £10,000 was offered by the Australian Government, he was determined to be the first to fly from Europe to Australia, despite not being eligible to win the prize.

Poulet chose Jean Benoist as his mechanic because they had flown together before and Poulet had previously paid tribute to his abilities. They almost made it but had to abandon the attempt in Burma due to bad conditions and mechanical problems.

After he abandoned his attempt to be the first to fly from France to Australia, Poulet spent a great deal of time in Asia. His reputation as a pilot was spreading, and in 1924 he was appointed aviation advisor to the Chinese Government at the invitation of Marshall Chang Tse Ling, a position that he held until 1935.

After the attack on Pearl Harbour in 1941 the Japanese invaded Indo-China and Poulet joined the resistance and became one of their leaders before being captured and imprisoned in a camp at Chapta in Tonkin province. At the end of the war Poulet returned to France, but by 1948 was back in Indo-China where the Government appointed him Chief Engineer of the

Fleet Air Force. His contract ended when he was sixty-five and he returned to France on Christmas Eve 1954.

The king of Cambodia requested his return but Poulet turned the request down, (which must have come as a shock to the king) preferring to spent his retirement in the tourist resort of Nice, in the country of his birth. Although retired, Poulet joined the Aero Club of Nice and became their president in March 1958. He died at the home of a friend on the 9th August 1960 at the age of seventy, one of France's most honoured and celebrated aviation pioneers.

## *The Aircraft*

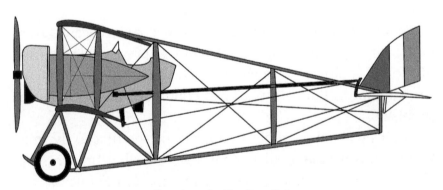

**Drawing of a Caudron G 4**

While the Caudron G 3 was a reliable reconnaissance aircraft, it was unable to carry a useful bombload, and owing to its design, it was also difficult to fit with useful defensive armament. In order to solve these problems, the manufacturers designed the G 4, a twin-engined development of the G.3, first flying in March 1915.

While the G.4 had a similar pod and boom layout to the G.3, it had two Le Rhone rotary or Anzani 10 radial engines mounted on struts between the wings, instead of a single similar engine at the front of the pilot's cockpit. This allowed for an observer come gunner position to be fitted in the nose section, while the additional power allowed it to carry a bombload of 100 kg. The wingspan was also increased and the tailplane was fitted with four rudders instead of the G3s two. The G.4 was one of the few twin-engine aircraft to be able to fly with one engine stopped.

With two engines and a large wing area, the G.4 had enough power to break altitude records, and in May 1915, Etienne Poulet broke the altitude record with 3 passengers, reaching a height of 5.850 m (19.226 ft). In Italy, on the 9th November 1916, the Italian aviator Guido Guidi set a world absolute altitude record, reaching a height of 26.083 ft (7.950m).

A total of 1358 G.4s were produced in France, while a further 51 examples were produced by the A.E.R. company in Italy and 12 were built in Britain by the British Caudron company.

As the first twin-engine machine to enter service with the French military in November 1915, the Caudron G 4 was used to carry out bombing raids deep behind the front line, even being used to attack targets as far away as Germany, but increasing losses led to its withdrawal from day bombing missions by the French in the autumn of 1916.

A Coudron G 4 being prepared for take-off

The British Royal Naval Air Service (RNAS) also used the G.4 as a bomber, receiving 55, of which twelve were licence-built by the British Caudron company and the remainder supplied from France.

Although it was finally replaced in RNAS service by the Handley page 0/100 aircraft in the autumn of 1917, the Italian G.4s proved to be very successful in operating in the mountainous Alpine arenas, where its good altitude capabilities proved useful, and it was also used by the Imperial Russian Air Force for reconnaissance purposes.

The machine used by Poulet in his attempt to fly from Paris to Australia had two additional fuel tanks installed between the wings to give it greater flight duration.

The Flight

Etienne Poulet not only worked for the Caudron aeroplane company as a test pilot, he had actively promoted the Caudron aircraft in aerobatic displays as far afield as Germany, Swizerland and Austria, but despite his repeated requests, no financial help was given towards his attempt by either the French Government or the Coudron company itself.

The project was therefore carried out at Poulet's own expense, with the support of industrialist Paul Plouvier and journalist Jean Lhermit. Desperate for at least some sponsorship, Etienne Poulet reluctantly agreed to cover his plane with advertisements for the engine manufacturers Gnome and Rhone, as well as for the brand of varnish that covered the canvas of the aircraft. The two fuel tanks also carried inscriptions as well as the upper wing.

After two unsuccessful attempts to get started from Villa Coubblay near Paris on the 12th and 13th October 1919, when on both occasions they were forced to return, one due to fog and the other engine trouble, Poulet and Benoist finally got away at 6.57 a.m. on Tuesday the 14th After dropping a wreath over Lyons, bearing the message, *"A mon ami Védrines"*, they landed at Fréjus, a small town just outside Paris at 2.p.m.

Poulet had notified the Australian press of his intention to beat the official race entrants to Australia, and had requested that fuel and oil be made available to him at certain locations when he reached Darwin.

Although Poulet and Benoist were not official entrants, it is to their considerable credit that the organisers immediately replied, announcing that the necessary supplies would be made available and wishing them a safe landing on Australian soil, even though their arrival ahead of official competitors would have been a major blow to the Australian Government.

Poulet and Benoist starting their journey from Paris

Reading stories about Poulet in the press, the Australian people recognised and admired the fact that he was sacrificing his own money and risking his life to help the family of a deceased friend and fellow aviator.

Poulet and Benoist left Fréjus intent on flying all the way to Rome but strong winds were buffeting the light aircraft, making flying conditions very difficult. Poulet decided to land near Genoa instead and hoped for better conditions the next morning.

The 16th October was indeed a brighter day but they still had to contend with heavy snow when crossing the Apennines. The little Caudron made it however and they landed safely at the Centocelle Aerodrome near Rome at 10.15 a.m.

With another early start the next morning and once again encountering bad weather, the Coudron managed only 160 miles before snow forced it to land at Naples. Poulet was understandably frustrated by the slow progress they were making and attempted to leave Naples the next morning despite the weather, but was forced to turn back. The same thing happened on the 19th, however their third attempt to leave proved more successful and they finally managed to fly safely across the South of Italy.

On route to Salonika the little Coudron once again encountered bad weather, but this time the sleet and snow were accompanied by a strong gale that carried them north into Albania. Fortunately they managed to locate and land at the Taviago Aerodrome near the town of Valona, where the weather forced them to remain for an agonising eight days. It was not until the 29th October that they left Valona and made it to Salonika. The next day was another early start and they were forced to fly at a height of a little over 300 feet due to heavy rain and poor visibility. Despite the poor conditions, they nevertheless managed to reach the Turkish capital of Constantinople just ahead of the dark at 5 p.m.

Taking the opportunity to rest for a day, they left Constantinople on the 1st November. The flight across Turkey was completed in small steps, landing first at Afyonkarahisar, before pushing on to Konya in the Salt Desert, and then Adana, where then planned to refuel. Unfortunately, the expected fuel supply was not there and Poulet was forced to take the chance that there was enough fuel left in the tanks to reach Aleppo. They say that fortune favours the brave, and this was certainly the case for Poulet and Benoist, for when the little Caudron touched down at Aleppo, they found that there were barely two litres of fuel remaining in the tanks.

They reached Baghdad at mid-day on the 5th November after following the Euphrates River out of Syria and left again the following morning to cover the 450 miles to Bushire. The next day they followed the coast of the Persian Gulf to Bandar Abbas. Here, they laid up for a day and Benoist carried out an overhaul of the Coudron's engines before leaving on the 9th, and flying down the Gulf of Oman to Char Bahar, just thirty miles short of what is now the Pakistan border.

Up until now, things had gone reasonably well for the Frenchmen, so it seems a little surprising that the Coudron's engines should choose to play up at that point, so soon after Benoist's overhaul. Poulet however, reasoning that better repair facilities would be available in India, decided to push on early the next morning.

They crossed the border into what was then India, (now Pakistan) but after progressing only as far as Pussni in the Indus Valley, they were forced to land. This was not, as it turned out, the safest of places to put down. The natives of the region had never seen an aircraft before and, it would seem, viewed the men who emerged from it as a threat and attacked them.

Fortunately for Poulet and Benoist their attackers arsenal did not contain firearms, so a couple of shots from their revolvers quickly repelled them. The threat posed by their hostile visitors nevertheless meant that while the two airmen worked to repair their aircraft, they also had to keep a lookout, fully expecting their attackers to return, possibly with reinforcements and more effective weapons.

During the night they had to take it in turns to keep watch, and even at dawn, when they commenced work on the Coudron once again, constant vigilance was needed. The heat during the day was such that, between mid-day and mid-afternoon, they had to shelter from the direct summer sun and work was impossible, so once again they took turns to keep watch during another anxious night.

This second night their fears were realised and they were attacked twice during the hours of darkness. Fortunately, the hostile natives still only used primitive weapons and were once again easily dispersed with a few pistol shots into the dark. The greatest danger came from a flaming torch that was thrown towards the Coudron, however the Frenchmen were able to get to it before it caused any damage. Although there were no further attacks during the remainder of the night, I doubt that much sleep was had by either Poulet or Benoist.

Work began again as soon as it was light enough and the repairs were finally completed before the heat of the day became intolerable. It was now the 12th November and the relief the two airmen must have felt at being able to take to the air again and head for Karachi is not difficult to imagine.

Our intrepid pair reached Karachi at 3.30 p.m. after covering the 100 miles from Pussni, where their journey could so easily have ended in disaster. New engines had been sent from Lahore and Poulet and Benoist set about installing them, unconstrained by the restrictions placed on the official entrants, that would have prevented them from changing a complete engine. They were also waiting for the arrival of some new maps, as Poulet had changed his mind about which route to take to Calcutta. He now planned to take the north-east route via Delhi instead of going south as originally intended.

They were falling behind their schedule with delay after delay and now, possibly because of nights spent in the open, Benoist was struck down with malaria. Whether Poulet ever considered continuing the journey without his valued mechanic is unknown, but given what we know of the man, it seems unlikely that he would ever have left a sick partner behind. In the end, Benoist recovered quickly and the pair took off from Karachi on the 18th November bound for Nasirabad, their one stop before Delhi.

Before they changed the engines at Karachi, apart from the trouble that had forced them down at Pussni, the Coudron had given them little cause for concern, but on landing at Nasirabad they discovered that the oil tank had sprung a leak, and while carrying out repairs on that, other things were found that also needed attention.

It wasn't until the 24th of November that they managed to get away from Nasirabad. Their destination aerodrome at Delhi was newly built and they arrived safely at 3.20 p.m. to be greeted by R.A.F. officers, including the Commanding Officer in India, Brigadier-General N.D.K. MacEwan.

After a night being wined and dined by the R.A.F. and after a good nights sleep, Benoist refuelled the Coudron with 100 gallons of petrol and 10 gallons of oil early the next morning. Just before they departed for Allahabad news reached them of Ross's arrival at Karachi. the Vickers Vimy with its powerful Rolls-Royce engines was close behind them and, barring accidents, was almost certain to overtake them soon.

They left Delhi at dawn and landed at Allahabad just after two in the afternoon, half expecting to be joined by Ross and his team at any moment. Poulet and Benoist left Allahabad at 7 a.m. on the 26th November and covered the 450-mile flight to Calcutta without incident.

Despite now constantly looking over their shoulders, and the threat of being overtaken, they took the decision to stay over for one day in Calcutta, overhauling the Coudron before flying over the Bay of Bengal Akyab in Burma. It must have been something of a relief to leave Calcutta the next morning at 8.00 a.m. without any sight of the Vimy and to land at Akyab safely. Now, even if they were to be beaten to Australia, theirs would still be the first aircraft to land in Burma, so they had achieved one first.

There was great excitement at the arrival of Poulet and Benoist and the Burmese were unsure just what to make of the airmen, especially when four more turned up the next day in the form of Ross and the Vimy team.

Poulet was still in Akyab when Ross arrived, and it dashed any remaining hope that he would be the first to Australia. It is a strong indication of the Frenchman's character, that despite what must have been a huge personal disappointment, Poulet was nevertheless determined to push through the crowd and be the first to congratulate Ross and his team on their achievement.

The two men had agreed to leave together for Rangoon but maintenance of the Vimy took longer, and as the Caudron was a slower machine anyway, Poulet actually took off an hour before the Vimy, but still arrived at the racecourse in Rangoon one hour after the faster machine.

Both teams were greeted and entertained by the Lieutenant-Governor of Burma, Sir Reginald Craddock and Lady Craddock and once again plans were made for them to leave together and it was hoped this time that the Vimy could fly slowly enough to enable them to fly together as far as Bangkok.

The Vimy took off first the next morning and circled the airfield waiting for Poulet to follow, but the Caudron seemed reluctant to start, so after twenty minutes Ross reluctantly headed for Bangkok alone.

Only a few minutes after the Vimy had left, the Coudron's engine decided it was time to cooperate and started up. They made good progress then until they reached the mountains where they encountered thick mists, and although the Vimy had been able to fly above them, the Caudron wasn't. Fearing that they would lose their way Poulet reluctantly returned to Rangoon. Things then went from bad to worse for Poulet and Benoist when the next morning both tyres burst when commencing take off. The next day, the 4th December, they managed to get airborne but were plagued by engine trouble and had to return yet again. After overhauling the engines, they finally managed to leave Rangoon behind them on the 8th December and landed at Moulmein.

Leaving Moulmein on the 9th bound for Bangkok some 260 mile distant, bad weather over the mountains that formed a part of the boundary between Burma and Thailand, plus a cranked piston and a broken propeller, forced them to return to Moulmein and brought the gallant efforts of the French aviators to a sad and disappointing end.

Ross landed in Darwin the next day and the fate of Poulet and Benoist was largely forgotten by all but the French. The cost of the expedition had left the Frenchmen broke, but Poulet was not without friends and admirers back home. The French rallied round their hero and raised enough money, now with the assistance of the Caudron factory, to buy the brave aviators a new machine.

Poulet was reported to be overwhelmed when news reached them in Burma on the 2nd January 1920 and they were determined to complete the flight to Australia in the new plane when the weather improved later in the year. To this end they left Rangoon on the 5th bound for Marseilles by sea.

After returning to India with the new plane they set about assembling and testing it before announcing that the latest Caudron was more than up to the task, and even hinted that they may well have beaten Ross had they been using the new aircraft then.

In order to satisfy himself of the suitability of landing sites, Poulet travelled east by boat to Kalidjati, Sourabaya, Bali and Lombok in Timor. After returning to Rangoon Poulet and Benoist left in the new Caudron on the 28th May 1920.

The reason for what happened next is unclear. They arrived in Batavia, Java, on the 13$^{th}$ July, apparently having abandoned any attempt to be the second to reach Australia, which they could so easily have been, as Ray Parer didn't arrive in the DH 9 until the 2$^{nd}$ August. All that we do know is that from that time on Poulet spent a great deal of his life in Asia.

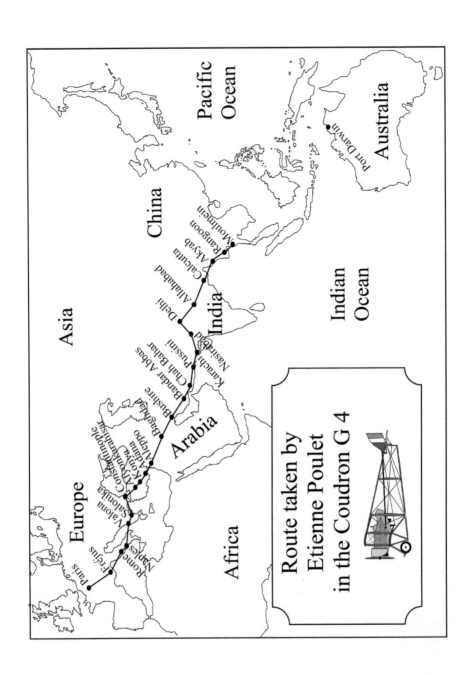

Route taken by
Etienne Poulet
in the Coudron G 4

# Chapter 4

# The Alliance P.2
# Team

The Alliance team consisted of Lieutenant Roger M. Douglas, MC. DCM. as pilot and Lieutenant J. S. Leslie Ross as navigator, radio operator and relief pilot.

### Lieutenant Roger M. Douglas (1894-1919)

Lieutenant Douglas was born in June 1894 at Charters Towers. Queensland to Walter Douglas, a miner and Alice Douglas, née Gratten.

As a youth he was a keen athlete and boxer, becoming the holder of both the Queensland lightweight and welterweight titles. Before the outbreak of war in 1914 he was employed by the Northern Miner newspaper and later the Townsville Daily Bulletin as a linotype operator. He also served as a citizen soldier in the 1st Australian Garrison Artillery and on the outbreak of war he spent six months on duty at Thursday Island in the

Torres Strait and is located approximately 39 kilometres north of Cape York Peninsula in far north of Queensland.

Lieutenant Roger Douglas

On 11<sup>th</sup> may 1915 he enlisted as a private in the Australian Imperial Force and he saw action in Gallipoli from 11<sup>th</sup> July 1915 until the evacuation in December, during which time he was promoted to corporal and then sergeant.

In March 1916 his battalion was shipped to France and he transferred to the 7<sup>th</sup> Machine-gun Company. During an action at Poziéres in August, he rallied part of the infantry who were without leaders and disorganised and guided them over the captured positions under heavy fire before helping to repel a counter attack. His bravery was rewarded with a second lieutenant's commission and a Distinguished Conduct Medal. He was promoted to Lieutenant on 25<sup>th</sup> November.

Douglas was awarded the Military Cross on the 28thh December 1917 in recognition of his bravery in action at Polygon Wood in the September of that year and he left the Machine-gun Company in November to join the Australian Flying Corps. He began his training in Reading, England in March 1918 and received his wings on the 5<sup>th</sup> May. He was appointed as an instructor with the 5<sup>th</sup> Australian Training Squadron at Minchinhampton, where he stayed until the end of the war, never actually flying in combat.

On his return to Australia he intended a career in civil aviation and he became engaged to a Miss Mabel Wooley shortly before the start of the race to Australia, in preparation for which he returned to England early, in order to take a special course in navigation at Andover, Hants.

## *Lieutenant J. S. Leslie Ross (1895-1919)*

Lieutenant Leslie Ross

Lieutenant J. S. Leslie Ross was born in Moruya, New South Wales where he also attended public school until 1909. On leaving school he worked as a telegraph messenger for the General Post Office for six years, after which he joined the Pacific Cable Board as a radio telegraphist.

Ross enlisted in the Australian Imperial Force, which had been formed on 15th August 1914, following Britain's declaration of war on Germany. His application was rejected at first, despite his being a qualified cable operator, but he persisted and was finally excepted on the 31st July 1916.

Trained as a radio operator he sailed for England with reinforcements for Number 2 Squadron of the Australian Flying Corps. After receiving his pilot's certificate at Oxford in 1916 he was appointed 2<sup>nd</sup> Lieutenant on 10<sup>th</sup> October 1917 and for three months was given the task of ferrying aircraft from England to the Australian Squadrons in France.

Promoted to Lieutenant on 20<sup>th</sup> January 1917 he re-joined Number 2 Squadron and saw action in France. In a dog-fight over Douai involving five Australian aircraft and eleven German machines, Ross, flying a SE5, was badly wounded in the thigh. Losing copious amounts of blood from his wound and obviously in a great deal of pain, as well as being in danger of losing consciousness, he nevertheless managed to return to the airfield and land safely.

After receiving hospital treatment, he was invalided back to England, but instead of re-joining his squadron he went on to study navigation at Andover.

## The Aircraft

The Alliance P2 was a single engine biplane fitted with a Napier Lion 450 h.p. 12-cylinder engine. With a crew of two, it had a wingspan of 53 ft and an overall length of 33 ft 6 in and a maximum speed of 140 mph. It had been developed from the Alliance P2 Seabird which had originally been designed as a transatlantic aircraft, but after Alcock and Brown's successful crossing, the company looked for other ventures with which to advertise and prove their aircraft.

The company had been formed in 1918 in response to pressure for aircraft manufacture. Samuel Waring, the owner of the furniture manufacturer Waring & Gillow together with the Nieuport and General Aircraft Company, formed the Alliance Aeroplane Company.

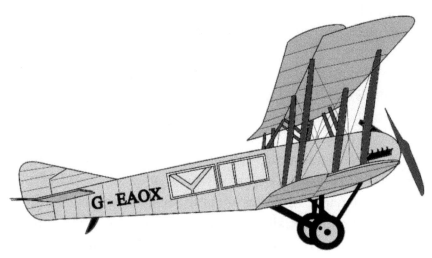

Drawing of the Alliance Endeavour

The main factory was located at Hammersmith but in order to obtain a suitable airfield the new company took over the Ruffy, Arnell and Baumann Aviation Company along with their premises at Acton Aerodrome.

In the last year of the First World War, the Alliance Aeroplane Company assisted in the building of several hundred biplanes and triplanes for the de Havilland and Handley-Page aircraft companies.

The first aircraft to bear the Alliance name was the last product of the old Ruffy, Arnell and Baumann company, their Elementary Trainer, which was subsequently improved and renamed the Alliance P.1.

After the end of the war the company turned to producing civil aircraft. They engaged the services of J.A. Peters, designer of the Robey-Peters Fighting Machine and produced a long distance machine, the P.2 Seabird which made a record non-stop flight to Madrid in July, 1919,

Although the factory remained in the hands of Waring & Gillow until 1945, the Alliance company never recovered from its failure in the Britain to Australia race and closed in 1920.

The aircraft, named after Captain Cook's vessel the Endeavour, was 37ft. in length and had a wingspan of 53ft. The petrol tank occupied the whole of the space between the propeller and the airmen's cabin, which was situated well back in the fuselage and fitted with dual controls, adjustable windows and leather chairs. Lieutenant Ross' seat was in front of the instrument panel while Lieutenant Douglas manipulated the controls from a specially constructed swivel chair just behind him. The rest of the cabin was fitted out with small cupboards containing emergency equipment and general provisions, including aspirin, quinine, drinking water, fire-extinguishers, cablegram forms, rations for five days and two revolvers, one of which had been taken by Douglas from a captured German officer in France.

## The Flight

The aircraft was finally tested at Acton aerodrome on October 30th when in accordance with the contest's regulation, officials of the Royal Aero Club attached distinctive marks and seals to the aircraft.

Many cables and farewell messages were recieved by the airmen prior to their departure, including one from the Aide de Camp to His Majesty the King and Commander of the Australian Imperial Force, General Sir W. R. Birwood, G.C.M.G., K.C.B., K.C.S.I., D.S.O. which read, "*I need hardly say how very sincerely and heartily I wish you all possible success. You know all the difficulties and dangers of the route, but you are no more daunted by these than your brother officers were by the perils of war. Go on boys, win over the forces of air and space. It is such men who have made the British Empire. Good luck. I hope to see you in Australia and congratulate you on the success won by real brave men.*"

The aircraft took off from Acton at 7.30 a.m. on 31st October and touched down briefly at Hounslow, the official starting point, before heading off for Italy. Bad weather, including fog in the Channel compelled them to return and start again on 13th November.

In the interim period it was reported that there had been a slight crash, necessitating the replacement of a section of the aircraft's chassis. Initially the designer of the aircraft, Mr J. A. Peters said in a sworn statement that the crash in question had happened during the preliminary flight on 31st October. However there is some confusion over the date, as it was later reported that the crash had occurred on the 9th November. Whichever date is correct, it seems likely that this was the reason for the almost two-week delay in starting.

Tragically, during its second attempt, the Alliance crashed soon after take-off on the 13th November in an orchard in Surbiton after only a few minutes into the flight. Ross was killed outright in the crash and Douglas died soon after of his injuries.

The Endeavour before take-off

One eye witness to the fatal crash stated that the aircraft had disappeared into low cloud, only to reappear a few minutes later flying at between 500 to 1000 feet before going into a spin, then straightening out before another spin that ended in a crash, only some 6 miles from Hounslow.

The aeronautical correspondent for the Times, an authority on aviation at the time wrote, *"The cause of the machine's fall is unknown and probably never will be known. Something serious happened at Surbiton. The machine steadily lost speed and the working of the engine became intermittent. The airmen seemed to be seeking a place to land. Suddenly the machine nose-dived, felling a large apple tree. Lieutenant Ross was thrown through the cabin roof and was found seven yards from the machine, dead. Lieutenant Douglas was extricated from the debris, but died shortly afterwards, without regaining consciousness. Stores of food, petrol tins and spare parts were strewn round the shapeless wreckage of the machine.*

*It is not the purpose of this article to touch on the many distressing scenes which followed the catastrophe. Lieutenant*

*Douglas' fiance, Miss Mabel Woolley, would, not unnaturally conceive a spirit of bitterness against the machine itself and against everybody concerned with its construction and, in the circumstances, her comments during the progress of the inquest may be accepted as those of one distracted with grief at the sudden tragic loss of her affianced husband.*

*Suffice it that the jury returned a verdict of accidental death, no blame being attached to the Alliance Company, designers and builders of the aeroplane, or to the makers of the engines, Messers.D. Napier & Sons,Ltd.*

*The generally accepted theory is that of the designer, Mr.J.A. Peters i.e., that the machine came out of the cloud in a spin, with the engine shut off, and that the pilot (Lieutenant Douglas) put her nose down in order to sraighten out, but had insufficient altitude in which to right himself.*

*On the question of overloading, it should be noted that the Endeavour weighed slightly more than two tons and was lighter by some 400 pounds than the machine in which Mr. Peters had attained a height of 13,000 feet on his London Madrid flight.*

*An examination of the wreckage and stripping of the engine showed no mechanical defect. In considering the effect of cold or snow (which has been publicly offered by two prominent Sydney airmen as a possible cause of engine failure) attention is directed to the accompanying description of the 450 h.p. Napier "Lion" engine, with which the wrecked machine was fitted. In this technican description, which appeared some months ago in a British aeronautical journal of high repute, it is stated that special attention had been given to the heating of the carburettors, the water jackets being carried down and round the throttles themselves to prevent them from freezing at high altitude."*

The funeral of both men took place at Brookwood Cemetery on the 17th November and a large crowd attended. The A.I.F. (Australian Imperial Force) was represented by Colonel

Durrant who led a team of officers acting as pall bearers.  Three volleys were fired over the graves and an Australian bugler sounded the Last post.

Lieutenant
Roger M. Douglas M.C.  D.C.M.

Lieutenant
J. S. Leslie Ross

**Graves of Douglas and Ross at Brookwood Cemetery**

# Chapter 5

# The Martinsyde A1 Team

The Martinsyde team consisted of Captain Cedric E. Howell and Air Mechanis 2nd Class George Henry Fraser.

### *Air Mechanic George Henry Fraser*

Air Mechanic G. H. Fraser

George Fraser, from Coberg, Victoria, was acting as Captain Howell's mechanic for the flight.

Fraser's exact date of birth is not given in the sources available, but he is variously stated to have been either 39 or 40 years old at the time of his death. He was the child of Robert Fraser (died 27 March 1894, aged 46) and Mary Fraser (died 15 March 1937, aged 92). He was born in Macorna, Victoria, Australia and attended Macorna State School. On leaving school, Fraser became a bicycle and motor mechanic and worked for several years in his brother William Fraser's car import firm, Messrs Fraser and Willsford of Sydney, who were the representatiives there for the Sunbeam Motor Car Co. Ltd. Australia, where he was residing at the time of his enlistment in 1917. He sailed to England later that same year with reinforcements to the A.F.C.

After service with No1 Bombing Squadron he learnt to navigate while on a course at Andover, after which he was employed by Martinsyde Ltd., the manufacturers of the aircraft he was now in, and the Rolls-Royce aero engine factory.

In written correspondence with his brother in Sydney, he mentioned the likelihood that he would accompany Captain Howell on the flight to Australia. Fraser was unmarried at the time of his death.

## Captain Cedric Ernest Howell D.S.O., D.F.C., M.C.

Captain Howell was born in Adelaide in January 1896 and was educated at the Church of England Grammar School, Melbourne. He initially trained as a draughtsman while holding a commission in the 49th Cadet Battalion, Citizens Military Forces. His first attempt to join up at the outbreak of war was unsuccessful due to his age but he was finally accepted into the Australian Imperial Forces as a private in 1915.

He saw action in Gallipoli as a sniper before contracting malaria, but once recovered sailed for France and served with the 46th Battalion at the Somme.

**Captain Cedric Howell**

In 1917 he was selected for service with the R.F.C., soon to become The Royal Air Force, where he received his training at Durham and later at Port Meadow, Oxford. From Oxford he was sent to the R.F.C. training ground at Yatesbury near Calne in Wiltshire for the completion of his training which was on Airco D.H. 5s.

He flew solo for the first time on 24th July 1917 and his instructor, Captain Geoffrey F. Hughes described him as, "*a very good chap, exceedingly promising and possessing tremendous self-confidence.*"

After his training had finished, he served in Italy, where he won both his M.C. and D.F.C. in the September of 1918 flying a Sopwith Camel, a D.S.O. followed in October.

A report about Captain Howell in the London Gazette dated 29th October 1918 reads, "*This officer recently attacked in company with one other machine, an enemy force of 15 aeroplanes, and succeeded in destroying four of them and bringing down one out of control. Two days afterwards he destroyed another enemy machine, which fell in our lines, and on the following day he led three machines against 16 enemy scouts, destroying two of them. Capt. Howell is a very gallant and determined fighter who takes no account of the enemy's superior numbers in his battles.*"

Captain Howell was a recognised "Ace" having been credited with having shot down thirty-two enemy aircraft as well as numerous kites and balloons.

Captain Howell had married while in Great Britain and on the day of Howell and Fraser's departure, his new wife was already on her way to Australia aboard the SS *Orsova*. It was Captain Howell's hope that he would overtake the Orsova near Naples and salute by flying a circuit around her, but I have not seen any reports from any witnesses that he managed to do so, or if he did, that anybody saw it.

THE AIRCRAFT

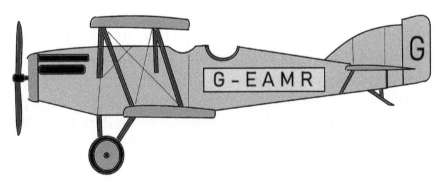

Drawing of the Martinsyde type A

The company was first formed in 1908 as a partnership between H.P. Martin and George Handasyde and known as Martin & Handasyde. Their No.1 monoplane was built in 1908–1909 but although it succeeded in lifting off the ground it was wrecked in a gale.

The company went on to build a succession of largely monoplane designs such as the Dragonfly shown here, although it was a biplane, the S1 of 1914, that turned Martin-Handasyde into a successful aircraft manufacturer.

In 1915 they renamed the company Martinsyde Ltd, and it became Britain's third largest aircraft manufacturer during World War One, with flight sheds at Brooklands and a large factory in nearby Woking.

The Martinsyde Type A that Captain Howell and his Air-mechanic Lieutenant Fraser were flying had a wing span of 43ft. 4in. It was powered by a single Roll-Royce Falcon engine producing 275 hp and a fuel tank capacity of 160 gallons.

The A 1 had performed well during tests at Brooklands, both as a land and seaplane, and they expected to make in the region of 8 miles per gallon at a steady 120 m.p.h. and have a flying range of some 1200 miles.

The intention was that on arrival at Calcutta, the aircraft was to be converted to a seaplane by the addition of floats which would be sent on in advance, as well as a spare set of undercarriage for their arrival in Darwin.

Martin-Handasyde 4B Dragonfly

## The Flight

On 4th December 1919, Lieutenant Fraser and Captain Howell boarded their aircraft as soon as the officials from the Royal Aero Club arrived. They reportedly did so without any ceremony or celebration and took off at 9.45 a.m. shouting "Ta-ta boys, we're off". The only people at the aerodrome to see them off were one or two reporters, some Royal Aero Club officials and some big-wigs from the Martinsyde organization.

The crew carried with them a number of letters for Australians which would make them, should they be successful, the first airmail flight from Britain to Australia. They were also in possession of messages wishing them a safe trip from H.R.H. Prince Albert and Mr Winston Churchill. The pair soon ran into poor weather however. The intention had been to reach Lyons but after a two-hour delay having a fuel pump replaced in Paris, they were forced to land the aircraft near Dijon, France later that day.

**The Martinsyde type A G-EAMR flow by Howell and Fraser**

Airborne again in the afternoon, when the weather improved, they flew over the Gulf of Genoa and arrived in Pisa, Italy the following day, where a replacement tail skid was fitted to the A1. A proper replacement skid was unavailable, so Fraser had to make one from what materials were to hand, something that he was well capable of doing. However, he was annoyed because both he and Howell had specifically asked the Martinsyde company to include a replacement skid as one of the spare parts to be taken with them.

The next day, 6th December, the duo managed to take-off from Pisa and landed in Naples at 3.30 p.m.

Sunday the 7<sup>th</sup> was a day of pouring rain and strong winds, but despite the adverse conditions the two intrepid airmen were determined to make it to Taranto. However, conditions only worsened as they pushed on and by the time they got to Salerno, both men were feeling airsick. Howell decided that to attempt a landing was too dangerous, so no doubt with heavy hearts, they made the decision to return to Naples.

After spending another night in Naples, they finally made it to Taranto. It was reported by the Air Ministry that on the 9th December, Howell and Fraser took off again in their Martinsyde plane from Taranto soon after noon, with the intention of reaching Athens.

What happened next has never been satisfactorily explaned.

Taranto to Athens is approximately 400 miles and should have taken them in the region of 4 hours, but nothing was seen of them until the Martinsyde was reported as being sighted flying over St George's Bay, Corfu at 20:00 that evening. Exactly what happened in the intervening hours remains a mystery, as Corfu itself is not much more than 150 miles from their starting point in Taranto. It was thought unlikely that they would have taken on a full tank of fuel for a journey of 400 miles and yet there are no known reports of any landings to refuel during the seven or eight hours their whereabouts is unknown, although the possibility that they did so can't be ruled out.

Officials from Martinsyde put forward the theory that they had zig-zagged over the true line of the course looking for landmarks in the misty conditions and eventually ran out of fuel.

What is known is that for some reason, Howell and Fraser attempted to execute an emergency landing at Corfu. They were however, unable to make it to the coast and were forced to attempt a landing in the sea.

It would further seem that the water landing was successful, at least from the point of view of the survival of the crew, as citizens in the area later reported that they heard cries for help coming from the sea that night, but a rescue attempt was not possible in the rough conditions. Both Howell and Fraser were tragically drowned.

There is a discrepancy between the dates given by different sources for the aircraft's departure from Taranto, and therefore the date of Howell's and Fraser's subsequent drowning. Some sources say the aircraft left on the 9th and others the 10th of December and this may be because of confusion over the time zones.

As soon as conditions allowed, a naval motor launch searched the area but no trace of the aircraft was found. Howell's body later washed ashore and was returned to Australia for burial, but Fraser's remains were never discovered.

The aircraft was later located in shallow water and an attempt was made to salvage it but bad weather intervened again and the plane broke up.

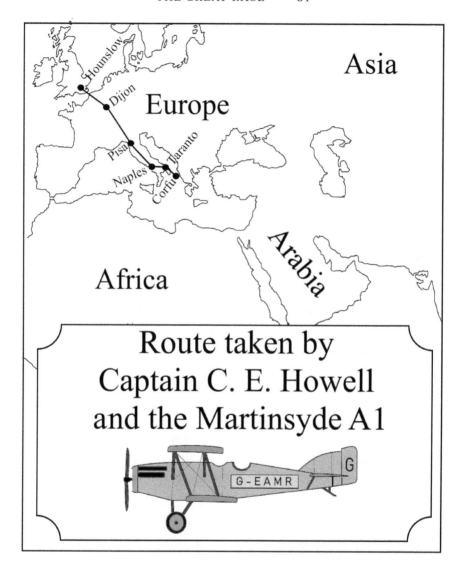

Route taken by Captain C. E. Howell and the Martinsyde A1

The news of the airmen's deaths was cabled to the SS Orsova but the decision was taken not to inform the new Mrs. Howell of the tragedy, on account of her being in poor health at the time. Captain Howell's father later met the ship at Adelaide to perform the heart-breaking task of informing his new daughter-in-law of her husband's death. Captain Howell's body was then brought from Corfu and buried at Heidelberg, Victoria.

Howell was accorded a funeral with full military honours, which took place at Warringal Cemetery, Heidelberg on 22nd April 1920, with several hundred mourners in attendance; his widow, parents and sister being chief among them. A firing party of the Royal Australian Garrison Artillery led the gun carriage bearing the coffin to the cemetery. Captains Adrian Cole, Frank Lukis and Raymond Brownell acted as pallbearers along with five other officers who had served in either the Royal or Australian Flying Corps.

On 12th February 1923, a stained-glass window dedicated to the memory of Howell was unveiled by General Sir Harry Chauvel at St. Anselm's Church of England in Middle Park. Howell had been a member of the congregation there in his youth. Following the closure of St. Anselm's in 2001, the window was moved to St. Silas's Church, Albert Park, which is now also the parish church for the former parish of St. Anselm.

Some months after the crash Captain Howell's father announced that he was not satisfied that the true circumstances of his son's death had been reported and called a number of public meetings.

He was curious as to why it had taken three days for news of the crash to be reported, as "*Corfu is only a small island which can be crossed in a day by motor car.*"

He went on to state, "*Our theory is that Captain Howell came safely to land but was murdered for his money. We believe that the body and the machine were then pushed into the sea. The fact that he was not wearing his Sidcote suit and high boots is strange.*" (*A Sidcote suit is the one-piece flying suit worn by pilots.*)

It was announced at one of the meetings that Captain Howell had £100 on him, as well as a considerable sum in credit notes when they left Taranto, but only 10/6d and no items of any value were found; and why, when Lieutenant Fraser's body was never located, was his wallet found five miles inland from the site of the accident?

Captain Howell's father also thought it strange that his son's pockets were found to be full of sand on arrival in Australia. "Surely, if a search had been made for any articles in the pockets, the sand would not have been replaced!"

To add to the confusion, Lieutenant Fraser's brother in Sydney had apparently received a cable saying that the pair had safely landed in Athens, although no evidence of the cable was ever disclosed. So could it be that Howell and Fraser did in fact land in Athens, and then decide for some reason to return to Taranto, maybe because they had left something important behind. Could it be that it was on this return journey that they crash landed? It would certainly explain the mystery of the excessively long time between the leaving Taranto and being spotted over St George's Bay, Corfu at 20:00 hours. Reports in the hands of Howell's father show that the Taranto to Athens leg was to be via Otranto, Valona, Corfu and the Gulf of Corinth and that contrary to earlier reports the pair had taken on 155 gallons of petrol at Taranto, almost a full tank.

During this time it would seem that Captain Howell's father also claimed that Captain Ross Smith had secured several advantages for his team that had disadvantaged other competitors. Howell had demanded a public enquiry into the terms of the race.

When he heard of these claims, Ross also called for an enquiry as a means of clearing his name stating "*I make every allowance for Mr. Howell's grief and mental disturbance due to the tragic loss of his son and have no wish to punish him by the bringing of a libel action against him*". Ross however receive a letter informing him that there would not be a public enquiry into the matter.

It seems that the exact events of that day and the circumstances of the airmen's deaths will always remain a mystery.

COMMONWEALTH OF AUSTRALIA.
415/1/1652.
DEPARTMENT OF DEFENCE.
MELBOURNE.

D.
No.

74751

12 OCT 1920

Dear Sir Ross Smith,

With further reference to your letter of 10th. September, I am directed to forward herewith for your information a statement of facts in connection with the subject matter submitted by Lieutenant Colonel R. Williams, and with which Senator Pearce's knowledge of events in London which came before him confirms.

I am to add that it is not proposed, in all the circumstances, to institute a public enquiry of the character which has been suggested.

Yours faithfully,

Secretary.

Captain Sir Ross Smith, K.B.E.,M.C., D.F.C.,
Hotel Australia,
Sydney,
New South Wales.

Letter to Captain Ross Smith. State Library of South Australia

# Chapter 6

# The Blackburn
# Kangaroo Team

The Blackburn Kangaroo team consisted of Sir George Hubert Wilkins, Lieutenant V. Rendle, Lieutenant D. R. Williams and Lieutenant Garnsey St. C. Potts.

The navigator was originally intended to be Charles Kingsford Smith but he withdrew and George Wilkins took his place.

*Sir George Hubert Wilkins*

The leader of the team, Sir George Hubert Wilkins (1888-1958), was a war correspondent and photographer, polar explorer, naturalist, geographer, climatologist and aviator.

He was born on 31 October 1888 at Mount Bryan East, South Australia, the thirteenth child of Henry Wilkins, a farmer, and his wife Louisa, née Smith. As a child, George experienced the devastation caused by drought and developed an interest in climatic phenomena. He studied engineering part time at the South Australian School of Mines and Industries and also pursued interests in photography and cinematography in Adelaide and Sydney. In 1908 he sailed for England to work for the Gaumont Film Co.

Captain Hubert Wilkins M.C.

As a newspaper reporter and cameraman, Wilkins visited many different countries and after learning to fly he experimented with aerial photography. Later in 1912 as a war correspondent and photographer he covered the fighting between the Turks and Bulgarians, and between 1913 to 1916 he was second-in-command on Vilhjalmur Stefansson's Canadian Arctic expedition. Wilkins became adept in the art of survival in polar regions, adding to his scientific knowledge and he conceived a plan to improve weather forecasting by establishing permanent stations at the poles.

He returned to Australia, and on 1st May 1917 he was commissioned as second lieutenant in the Australian Imperial Force (Australian Flying Corps). By August he had been transferred to the general list and was at Anzac Corps headquarters on the Western Front. Appointed official photographer in April 1918, he was tasked with providing "*an accurate and complete record of the fighting and other activities of the A.I.F.*" as a counterpart to Captain J. F. Hurley's propaganda work.

In June Wilkins was awarded the Military Cross "*for bringing in some wounded men*".

He was promoted to captain on 11 July after Hurley's departure and took charge of No.3 (Photographic) Sub-section of the Australian War Records unit. He routinely visited the front line for part of each day that troops were engaged in combat, and he periodically accompanied infantry assaults. During the battle of the Hindenburg line, on 29th September he organized a group of American soldiers who had lost their officers in an enemy attack and directed operations until support arrived. Awarded a Bar to his M.C., he was also mentioned in dispatches. The A.I.F. published his edited *Australian War Photographs: A Pictorial Record from November 1917 to the End of the War* (London, 1918).

After his participation in the Great Britain to Australia Air Race, Wilkins engaged in more polar exploration, and in 1920-21 he made his first visit to the Antarctic, accompanying J. L. Cope on his unsuccessful voyage to Graham Land. Wilkins next took part in Sir Ernest Shackleton's *Quest* expedition of 1921-22 on which he made ornithological observations.

While surveying and filming the effects of famine in the Soviet Union in 1922-23, the trustees of the British Museum asked him to proceed to tropical Australia and collect specimens of the rarer native fauna, principally mammals, and he published a book on his return entitled, *"Undiscovered Australia."*

In 1926 when a projected Antarctic expedition failed through lack of funds, he began a programme of Arctic exploration by air. The enterprise culminated in his great feat of air navigation: in April 1928, with Carl Ben Eielson as pilot, he flew from Point Barrow, Alaska, United States of America, eastward over the Arctic Sea to Spitsbergen (Svalbard), Norway. He was knighted in June, and awarded the Patron's medal of the Royal Geographical Society of London and the Samuel Finley Breese Morse medal of the American Geographical Society. His book, *Flying the Arctic* (New York, 1928), publicised the achievement.

On 30th August 1929 in the registry office, Cleveland, Ohio, Wilkins married Suzanne Evans, an Australian-born actress known by her stage name 'Suzanne Bennett' and although they were to remain childless, the marriage was a happy one with both parties pursuing their own careers.

Sir Hubert had carried out the first aerial explorations of the Antarctic in November 1928 and January 1929. While most of his discoveries were later shown to have been mistaken, his reconnaissance greatly influenced the course of all subsequent exploration in the area. He visited Antarctica again in 1930 and attempted the following year to reach the North Pole by taking a surplus United States Navy submarine, renamed *Nautilus*, under the pack-ice but the venture had to be abandoned due to a series of mechanical failures. Wilkins's account of the operation appeared in *Under the North Pole* (New York, 1931). In collaboration with Lincoln Ellsworth, he made four further expeditions (1933-34, 1934-35, 1935-36 and 1938-39) to the Antarctic continent. During 1937 and 1938 he played a major role in the search for the Russian aviator Sigismund Levanevsky who disappeared on a flight from Moscow to Fairbanks, Alaska.

At the outbreak of World War Two, he offered his services to the British and Australian governments, but was rejected on account of his age. Nevertheless he became involved in a number of missions for United States government agencies, visiting the Middle East, South-East Asia and the Aleutian Islands. From 1942 he was a consultant and geographer with the U.S. Army Quartermaster Corps which sought his advice on rations and equipment suitable for use in conditions of extreme cold. He held other defence-related scientific posts, and served in the U.S. Weather Bureau and the Arctic Institute of North America.

A fellow of the Royal Geographical Society and the Royal Meteorological Society (1923), Wilkins could be dismissive of

conventional scientific method. He was primarily a field explorer and pioneer who worked to a clear, long-range plan,
based on his conviction of the necessity for a world-wide
meteorological organization. Yet his curiosity drew him irre-
sistibly to new ideas and projects.

In 1955 he was granted an honorary D.Sc. by the University
of Alaska. Despite his solitary nature, he was a good mixer
and companion. Tall and athletic, he had physical drive and
courage to match his mental endurance, and he held deep reli-
gious convictions.

He died suddenly in his hotel room at Framingham, Mass-
achusetts, on 30th November 1958 and was cremated; four
months later his ashes were scattered from the nuclear submarine *Skate* at the North Pole and in 1966 a memorial plaque
was unveiled at Hallett, South Australia in his honour. Lady
Wilkins survived him and wrote affectionately of a husband
whose only contact with her for extended periods had been
through his letters.

## Lieutenant V. Rendle,

Lieutenant Valdemar Rendle, (Val) was born in Brisbane in
1897 and had always shown a keen interest in aviation. He was
a member of both the Gliding Club and the Courier Aeroplane
Clubs there.

At the outbreak of war in 1914 he immediately offered his
services to the Australian Flying Corps but was turned down
as he was only 17 at the time. In 1915 he sailed for England
with seven other Queenslanders and was accepted into the
Royal Flying Corps as a mechanic but also trained as a pilot
and gained his wings very quickly.

**Val Rendle in 1919**

For a while he was Acting Flight Commander and received his second star, becoming a Lieutenant, in March 1917. His experiences include working as a mechanic in an aircraft factory, being a test pilot and piloting the official aerial mail from London to Paris.

After the 1919 race he was rumoured to be planning a crossing of the Pacific from America to Australia, a prize of $50,000 being offered for such a venture by American millionaire Thomas H. Ince, but such attempts were discouraged by both the American and Australian authorities who considered them too dangerous. Rendle's plan had been to fly a seaplane from San Francisco to Hawaii, on to Samoa via Fanning Island and Palmyra, but nothing came of it in the end.

Rendle returned to England and found work in the household appliance business. At the start of World War Two he enlisted and served in Egypt. He died in Brisbane on the 11th August 1962 leaving a wife and three children.

## *Lieutenant D. R. Williams.*

Lieutenant Reginald (Reg) Williams was born in Wodonga, Victoria, in 1896 and moved to New South Wales in 1907 with his brother Percy, where they established a motorcycle garage at 22 Summer Street, in Orange, where the both enlisted.

Lieutenant D.R. Williams

A keen motorcyclist, Reg competed in many races. In January 1915 he received the highest award in the Melbourne to Sydney Motor Cycle Reliability Trial. Reg was the only competitor to complete the return journey, riding 1350 miles in eight days.

When the School of Aviation at Richmond was established Reg was one of the first cadets to enlist. Such was his aptitude for flying that Reg received his pilot's certificate after just seven hours of instruction. He remained at Richmond as an instructor until June 1917 when he was posted to England as part of the Australian Flying Corps. At number 30 Training Squadron in Ternhill, Shrewsbury he did a course flying Avro and Sopwith fighters, after which he was attached to number 7 Training Squadron at Leighterton, flying R.E.8's and then on to Winchester for final training. At 21 years of age Reg never reached the front line, but delivered new aircraft from England to France.

After the war he joined his friend Garnsey Potts at the Grahame White Aviation Works to work on the Kangaroo.

An accident at Suba Bay ended his involvement in the 1919 race from Britain to Australia and on the 8th December Williams returned to Sydney by ship, arriving on the 13th March 1920.

In partnership with his brother Percy, who had also seen service with the Australian Flying Corps, they formed the motorcycle business of P and R Williams and obtained the agency for A.J.S. and Velocette motorcycles. After a brief period away from the firm teaching flying and providing passenger flights, he married Mabel Lawson in May 1921, in the Methodist

Church at Canobolas.  As a married man he gave up flying and returned to the firm.

In 1939 he took a course in Royal Australian Airforce Administration and in 1940 was appointed C.O. of the Recruit Depot at Richmond.  After several moves around the country he was eventually appointed to his final position, that of C.O. of Number 2 Personnel Depot at Bradfield Park in April of 1944, before returning to civilian life in 1945 and retirement in 1959. He died in 1982 aged 86.

## *Lieutenant Garnsey St. Clair Potts.*

Lt. Garnsey Henry Meade St Clair Potts

Lieutenant Garnsey (Gar) H. M. St. Clair Potts was the second son of the Principal of Hawkesbury Agricultural College in New South Wales and was educated at King's College, Parramatta and Sydney Technical College.  When war broke out he was training as an engineer in the Australian Electric Lighting Company's works.

He joined the first group of trainees at the State School of Aviation in Richmond alongside Lieutenant Williams and others.  It was there that he obtained his pilot's certificate, before moving on to the Central Flying School at Point Cook, Victoria where he was granted a commission in the Australia Flying Corps on January 11<sup>th</sup> 1917.

In May of 1917, he joined Number 3 Squadron A.F.C. under Flight Commander Lieutenant Nigel B. Love and was stationed at Villers Bocage in France. Only one week later Potts returned to England as a gunnery officer with Number 7 Squadron where he saw out the rest of the war. After the hostilities, in 1919 he joined the Grahame White Aviation Company at Hendon where he studied aircraft construction until joining the Kangaroo team heading for Australia.

After the team's abandonment of the Britain to Australia flight he returned to Australia aboard the S.S. Bremen and started work for a newspaper in Brisbane before getting a job with Qantas Empire Airways in Sydney.

During the Second World War he became a Squadron Leader stationed at Number 1 Wireless Air Gunnery School, Ballarat, that was established on the 22nd April 1940 as part of the Empire Training Scheme. This scheme was to support RAF Bomber Command during WW2.

*Footnote*

Charles Kingsford Smith who was the original choice for navigator on the Blackburn Kangaroo team and whose place was taken by Captain Wilkins, later went on to make the first transpacific flight from the United States to Australia in 1928 after distinguishing himself in the First World War by being awarded the Military Cross for his gallantry in battle. He also made the first non-stop crossing of the Australian mainland, the first flights between Australia and New Zealand, and the first eastward Pacific crossing from Australia to the United States; and also made a flight from Australia to London, setting a new record of 10.5 days.

Charles Kingsford Smith

In 1935 Kingsford Smith and co-pilot John Thompson "Tommy" Pethybridge were flying the *Lady Southern Cross* overnight from Allahabad, India, to Singapore, as part of their attempt to break the England-Australia speed record, when they disappeared over the Andaman Sea in the early hours of 8th November. Despite a search for 74 hours over the Bay of Bengal by test pilot Eric Stanley Greenwood OBE, their bodies were never recovered.

## *The Aircraft*

Drawing of a Blackburn Kangaroo

The Blackburn Kangaroo had been developed as reconnaissance and torpedo attack aircraft, although it was mainly used as a conventional bomber operating from land bases. It could be easily identified by its slim fuselage and unusually large overhang of its upper wings.

Powered by two Rolls-Royce 250 hp Falcon 11 engines with four blade wooden propellers, the land plane had a pair of two-wheel undercarriage fitted under the engines.

Flown for the first time in December 1917 the first prototype Kangaroo was criticised during trials for its unsprung undercarriage and weak fuselage construction but these issues were addressed in the production aircraft that were fitted with wider, shock-absorbing main undercarriage legs and also fitted with the more powerful 275 hp Rolls-Royce Falcon 111 engines. The aircraft had a maximum speed of 107 m.p.h. and was listed as 5,284 lb. empty and 8,017 lb. when loaded.

Accommodation for a bomb-aimer and forward gunner was provided in an exposed cockpit in the extreme nose which was ahead of the separate open cockpit for the pilot. The rear gunner (who also served as wireless operator) was seated in a third cockpit aft of the wings.

The Admiralty purchased all nineteen production aircraft along with the prototype and delivered them to RAF Seaton Carew, from where they were used on several successful missions including the crippling of submarine UC70 that was later sunk by depth charges.

After the war eleven aircraft were sold to the civilian market, three of which were purchased by the Grahame-White Aviation Co Ltd. who enlarged the rear cockpits to accommodate seven passengers. These aircraft were used to give joy-rides to civilians with an eighth passenger occupying the nose cockpit.

In 1919 Blackburn set up The North Sea Aerial Navigation Co, later named The North Sea Aerial and General Transport Co Ltd. with eight surplus Kangaroo aircraft and the first (G-EAIT) was modified to carry seven passengers in an enclosed cabin. Unfortunately, this aircraft crashed shortly after its conversion on the 25$^{th}$ May 1925.

**G-EAIT with an enclosed passenger cabin**

The original prototype (ELTA) was given the civil registration G-EAOW and fitted out for the Britain to Australia race.

Also in 1925, North Sea Aerial and General set up a training school and four Kangaroos were fitted with dual control cockpits to provide twin engine training to RAF Reserve pilots.

## The Flight

Originally the crew of the Kangaroo was to be made up of Kingsford Smith, Cyril Maddocks, Lieutenant V. Rendle and Booker. Booker withdrew and Williams took his place, and then later Kingsford Smith left for America with Maddocks and their places were taken by Wilkins and Potts.

Apart from supplying the plane itself, the Blackburn company did not contribute financially to the venture, so apart from some support from the Shell fuel company while the they were in England, the team had to finance the attempt from their own funds.

Captain Williams is reported to have said that the accumulation of valuable scientific data and the removal of some of the difficulties of future flights to Australia was far more attractive to him than the cash prize of £10,000. Whether the rest of the crew shared his sentiments seems unlikely. However the onboard equipment included wet and dry bulb barometers, an aneroid barometer, course and drift indicators, a position finding device of his own design, and a density meter for measuring humidity. Numerous recording of meteorological variations were taken and recorded in a special log, compiled in accordance with the recommendations of the Air Force Research Committee. Cinematograph apparatus was also carried along with rifles for protection.

On 21st November 1919 the team left Hounslow, England, and after circling the airfield three times, obviously in jubilant mood, they headed for France on the first leg of their gruelling journey.

Reg recalled: "*It was bitterly cold all the time. On the first day out from England, we flew for about four hours in a snowstorm with no means of navigating, just a compass.*"

The crew conversed by sending notes to each other via a pulley and wire attached to the side of the plane and were constantly plagued by inclement weather, but finally managed to land at Romilly 62 miles east of Paris.

It must have been a huge disappointment the next morning when the crew rose to find everything covered in a deep blanket of snow. Departure on the next leg of their journey was delayed until the 25th November, but even then, they only made it as far as Lyons. Whether they were aware of the fact that the Vickers team had missed the worst of the bad conditions and were well in front of them I don't know, but it would certainly have added to their woes.

There was a shortage of fuel at Lyons which meant that they had to divert to Istres. From there they headed for Pisa but once again bad weather intervened and forced them to return to Istres. Leaving Istres for the second time on the 28th November, they landed safely at St. Raphael at 4pm.

Leaving St. Raphael at 9.30 a.m. on the 29th November they experienced engine trouble when passing over Antibes and were forced to make an emergency landing. Some reports say that the trouble was caused by sabotage that had occurred while they were in St. Raphael, and that wiring had been interfered with, causing a short circuit in the magneto, but there does not appear to be any evidence to support the claim. Despite this setback however, they still managed to get to Pisa that same day.

Whether, having lost so much time, the team ever considered declaring a false start and returning to Hounslow to restart the race is unclear. Certainly, there was nothing in the regulations to prevent them doing so, and it could have potentially cut days off their overall time, although they would no doubt have been expected to pay another £100 entry fee.

Desperate to make up for lost time, and despite a strong wind, they had the Kangaroo back in the air on the 30th November and managed to cover the 120 miles to Rome against the wind in a little under five hours.

It seemed that nothing was going to be easy for the team. Although leaving Rome on the 1st December they did not arrive in Taranto until the 3rd, having been forced to land at Capua to remove the magneto that was still proving troublesome.

They took off from Taranto on the 5th December heading down the coast of Greece to Suba Bay in Crete. The aerodrome was suffering the after effect of flooding, and despite a successful landing, the next morning saw the aircraft bogged down in mud. Bulgarian prisoners were brought in to dig the plane out of the mud and clean up the runway but it wasn't until the 8th of December that the Kangaroo team again made it into the air, but their troubles were far from over.

Some thirty or forty miles into their journey, Potts passed a note reporting that oil was leaking from the port engine and that the oil crankcase had broken off. It took a great deal of skill and courage to pilot a twin engine plane on only one engine. Easy enough today perhaps with modern aircraft, but back then the crew must have thought their chances of surviving the situation were slim at best, flying as they were over water.

Luck was with them for a change, and Rendle's skilful flying managed to get them back to Suba Bay. The aircraft was down to 800 ft however, so Rendle took the decision to turn on the port engine again despite its lack of oil, in the hope that it would function long enough to enable them to land safely. His gamble didn't pay off however, and the water jackets ruptured, sending fragments though the fuselage but luckily missing the crew.

The Kangaroo nose down in the ditch

A crash landing was inevitable and Rendle only just managed to clear the roofs of a row of houses as they came down heavily, bursting all four tyres. Still travelling forward at some speed, they were heading for a solid stone wall that surrounded the local mental hospital. Fortunately for all concerned there was a bank of earth and a ditch in front of the wall and this brought the Kangaroo to an abrupt halt, nose down and tail in the air. Miraculously none of the crew were injured apart from minor bruising. Unable to secure a new engine in a reasonable time, the difficult decision was taken to abandon the race, and a few days later they received the news that Vickers team had arrived in Darwin.

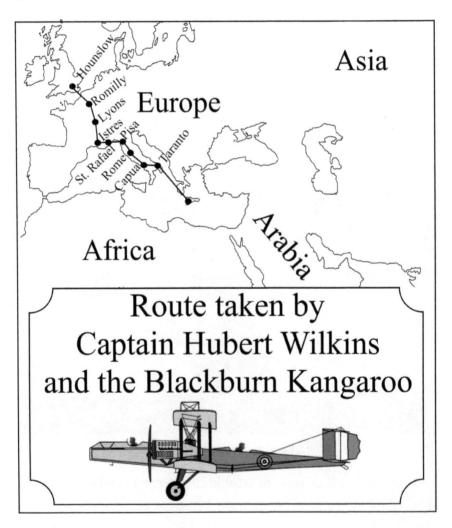

Route taken by
Captain Hubert Wilkins
and the Blackburn Kangaroo

# Chapter 7

# The Sopwith
# Wallaby Team

The crew of the Sopwith Wallaby consisted of Captain G. C. Matthews and Sergeant T. D. Kay of the Australian Flying Corps. they departed Hounslow on the 21st October. 1919

## Captain George Campbell Matthews

Born in South Australia, Captain George Matthews worked for the Australian shipping line, Howard Smith, and had gained a master's certificate as well as experience as a navigation officer. He enlisted in the Australian Light Horse on the 25th September 1914 and following service with the regiment in Gallipoli, he transferred to the Camel Corps serving in Egypt. After a few months with the Camel Corps he joined the Australian Flying Corps and trained as a pilot.

Captain George Campbell Matthews

Having gained his wings in Egypt and after being promoted to Lieutenant, he sailed to England to finish his training at Grantham, Lincolnshire. Whilst there, he took part in a mass flight of fifteen DH5 biplanes from Harlaxton in England to France. On the 21st October 1917, and was promoted to Captain.

Returning to England he was loaned to the Royal Air Force where his navigation experience and master's certificate were of use. His knowledge also enabled him to fit out the Wallaby with the very latest navigational equipment.

After the race and back in Australia he was one of the first to receive a licence under the Air Navigation Bill of 11th November 1920, and in 1923 he joined "Qantas" as a pilot.

On the 13th September 1923, Matthews crashed during a forced landing. The aircraft was badly damaged but Matthews himself was fortunate and walked away uninjured. He left Qantas in 1924 to join the Australian Mail Service, but later formed the Matthews Aviation Company to fly from Melbourne to Launceston and Hobart in a Saunders-Roe Cutty Sark, a four-passenger amphibious aircraft.

## Sergeant Thomas D. Kay

The son of Mr and Mrs T. Kay of Spring Mount, near Creswick, Victoria, Sergeant Kay had been an engineer in civilian life working for the firm of Ronaldson Brothers and Tippit in Ballarat, Victoria.

Sergeant Thomas D. Kay

He joined the Central Flying School at Point Cook, Victoria as a mechanic and sailed for England with Number 3 Squadron Australian Flying Corps on October 20th 1916.

After the hostilities of the First World War had ended, he started work at the Rolls-Royce aero factory in England and obtained his pilot's certificate while there. At the time of the race, both he and Captain Matthews were members of the Larkin-Sopwith Aviation Company of Australasia Ltd. of Melbourne and Sydney. Sergeant Kay died in 1963.

## The Aircraft

The Sopwith Aviation Company had originally intended to enter their Sopwith Dove for the race and for it to be flown by Herbert John Hinkler AFC, D.S.M. (1892-1933). Better known as Bert Hinkler and dubbed the "Australian Lone Eagle" he was a pioneer aviator and designer of early aircraft, who also became the first person to fly solo from England to Australia in 1928 flying an Avro Avian bi-plane. He died in an air crash near Florence, Italy in 1932 at the age of 39.

Sopwith Dove

The reason Hinkler and the Dove were withdrawn from the race probably had more to do with the fact that Hinkler really wanted to fly solo, rather than any shortcomings with the chosen aircraft. However the company did substitute the Wallaby in place of the Dove.

Drawing of a Sopwith Wallaby

The Wallaby was based on and closely reassembled an earlier Sopwith aircraft, the "Atlantic" that had been developed to be a transatlantic aircraft. The Wallaby resembled the Atlantic not only in appearance and dimensions, but also in having the same powerplant, a Rolls-Royce Eagle V111 V 8 engine, water cooled and producing 360 hp.

The Wallaby was 31 ft 6 in long with a wingspan of 46 ft. 6 in. It had a weight empty of 2,780 lb. and a gross weight of 5,200 lb., but the main differences between the two aircraft was that the Wallaby had three wing bays as opposed to the Atlantic's two, a wing bay being the area between supporting struts. The other differences were that the Wallaby dispensed with the extra fuel provision, the lifeboat and the jettisonable landing gear of the Atlantic.

It was a good deal more lightly loaded than the Atlantic, and carried 200 gallons of petrol instead of the almost 400 of its predecessor. The actual machine however was slightly heavier and stronger in construction. The arrangement of the cockpit had several features of special interest. The pilot's seat could be raised so that he was able to look out over the top of the fuselage or lowered and a lid pulled down over his head so that the occupants were entirely enclosed. The passenger's seat was movable, and there was a complete set of dual controls, the joy sticks being removable. The whole interior was quite roomy, and had windows of triplex glass. There was an air intake to bring fresh air to the occupants and windows at the side could be opened.

As well as the usual instruments such as compasses, and the airspeed meter, there was a turn-meter, which by recording the difference of air pressure on the two wing tips, told the pilot if he was keeping on a straight course when in mist or cloud; there was a flow meter, recording the rate of consumption of petrol; a spirit-level for sideways motion; an inclinometer for measuring the angle fore and aft; and an "azimuth mirror" for checking the compass by readings from the heavenly bodies on a system patented by Captain Matthews himself. Used in conjunction with a compass, this device enabled the operator to take celestial and terrestrial bearings. By means of a mirror and a lens, the azimuth mirror allows both the compass's cardinal points (direction), and the 'object' to be seen at the same time and in the same direction. The window below the pilot was marked in degrees so that he could observe the direction of drift.

**azimuth mirror in brass**

The Wallaby had strong connections with Australia, as the name would suggest. Not only was it built at Kingston-upon-Thames under the supervision of Australian, Harry Hawker, to compete in the 1919 race, but an associated company, the "Larkin-Sopwith Aeroplane Company" had been set up with offices in Melbourne in anticipation of both competition and commercial success.

## The Flight

On Tuesday the 21st October 1919, Captain Matthews and Sergeant Kay arrived at Hounslow aerodrome wearing their military uniforms. Officials of the Royal Aero Club together with a number of Australian and British officers were there to see them off on their epic journey.

Captain Matthews had on his person a letter addressed to His Excellency Sir Ronald Munro Ferguson, the Governor-General of the Commonwealth, from His Majesty King George V.

The official start was recorded as 11.44 a.m. and the Wallaby team were accompanied for the first few miles of their journey by Sopwith triplane, piloted by Mr Harry G. Hawker, the chief test pilot for Sopwith who later went on to co-found Hawker Aircraft with Tom Sopwith, Fred Sigrist and Bill Eyre. As Matthews and Kay were the first official team to leave England, their departure also marked the official start of the race, and even though Poulet had left France on the 14th and was well on his way, Matthews was confident that the Wallaby would have little trouble in overtaking the little Caudron G 4.

Captain Matthews' intention was to fly direct to Cologne but they ran into fog after covering approximately 100 miles and were forced to land at Marquise. Resuming the flight two days later on the 23rd October they reached Cologne, where they remained until 2nd November.

It was at Cologne also, that Matthews received a cable from the Australian Prime Minister, which read, *"Wish you and Sergeant Kay every success in your great adventure. Every one of your fellow citizens hopes that an Australian aviator may be the first to fly from England to Australia and so achieve what will easily be a world's record in aerial navigation. Want you to take no unneccessary risks, to plug on day after day doing your best, but do nothing foolhardy. If you cannot make Australia in 30 days never mind. The main thing is that an Australian should get here first. If you do that you need not worry. Good luck. Hughes."*

There is some speculation as to what exactly Hughes meant by his last statemant in the cable, "If you do that you need not worry". Does he mean that the £10,000 prize would be paid even if the first to arrive did so outside of the stipulated 30 days? We shall probably never know for sure, but it does seem likely. We do know the Hughes sent similer cables to the other contestants stressing that they should concentrate their efforts on safety rather than speed.

There was also some confusion about the reason for the long delay after reaching Cologne. Early reports stated that the aircraft had been damaged on landing, and that Sergeant Kay had been injured to such an extent that he would be unable to continue. However on the same day, a Sydney newspaper reported that they had mechanical trouble and were receiving help from the 3$^{rd}$ Wing of The Royal Air Force.

Whatever the case, the pair left Cologne on the 2$^{nd}$ November. They flew to Mayence, Germany, where they were further delayed until the 29$^{th}$ when they finally managed to land at Vienna. Much of Europe at that time was covered in snow and there was a good deal of dense fog around to add to their troubles.

Matthews and Kay left Vienna as soon as they could but were forced to land once again a good hundred miles short of Belgrade in what was then Yugoslavia. This part of Europe was still in a state of unrest after the war and bands of patriots and revolutionaries were still fighting. This was no place to be. Being in uniform and flying an aeroplane, it wasn't long before they were arrested as Bolsheviks and placed in a makeshift prison no bigger than 10 feet square. Here, rather than being treated as heroes, their captors were brutal, and they were fed on only bread and water and pig's fat. The two brave aviators were in fear for their lives, fully expecting to be put up against a wall and shot at any moment.

Even after four days they had been unable to convince their captors of their identity, or contact anyone in Belgrade that could vouch for them. When an opportunity to escape in dense fog presented itself, the two airmen willingly took the chance, despite the real possibility that they would be shot on sight if seen trying to escape, and the fact that the fog would make taking off extremely hazardous, even assuming they could reach their plane.

But luck was with them for a change. Most of their guards appeared to be drunk after a night of celebration, and they managed to locate the aircraft and start it quickly before their captors realised what was happening. Eventually the escaping pair were spotted, their captors no doubt being alerted by the sound of the aircraft's engines starting up, and several shots were fired at the departing Wallaby before it disappeared into the fog. Fortunately none of the rounds found their target.

Anxious, hungry and flying blind, their priority now was to find fuel, both for the aircraft and themselves. Breaking out the emergency rations to at least partially alleviate their hunger, they searched for the nearest airfield, hoping that there would be fuel for the aircraft and that the reception would be more friendly than the one they had recently encountered.

Fortunately, on the 11th December the fog cleared enough for them to spot the airstrip at Novisad, 45 miles short of Belgrade, when they were down to their last few gallons of petrol. Novisad was in the hands of the French who were only too pleased to help airmen, but unfortunately had no petrol.

Matthews caught the first train to Belgrade and made contact with a General Plunkett, but once again there was no petrol to be had. As luck would have it however, a French aviator landed at Belgrade while Matthews was there, and although very reluctant, General Plunkett and Matthews finally manage to persuade the pilot to part with sufficient fuel for the next leg of their journey.

By this time the aircraft was in need of a complete overhaul. Things had become so bad that a leak in the water-jacket had been repaired with chewing-gum mixed with asbestos powder and held in place with copper wire.

In spite of the bad state of repair of the Wallaby, and the stressed and tired condition of its crew, they nevertheless managed to land safely at Constantinople on the 23$^{rd}$ December where they heard the news that Ross and the Vickers Vimy team had arrived in Darwin. Despite the fact that the news must have come as a huge disappointment to them after all they had been through, Matthews and Kay cabled their congratulations to the winning team from the Turkish Capital.

The intention had been to leave on the 2$^{nd}$ January but they didn't manage to get away from Constantinople until the 14$^{th}$, flying the 500 miles to Aleppo, Syria. The journey took them over the mountains of Asia Minor where they had to fly at a height of 10,000 feet for more than two hundred miles, over territory where a forced landing would have been not just disastrous, but almost certainly fatal. It had been hoped that there would be a British presence in Aleppo to help, but this was not the case. It had been raining for a week in Aleppo and they were forced to stay until the 21$^{st}$ January, when they finally managed to get away and reached Baghdad that afternoon, relieved that at least they would now be able to carry out some much needed maintenance.

With the Wallaby now overhauled, the pair took off for Bushire, Persia (now Iran). After re-fuelling, the team left Bushire on the 3$^{rd}$ February with the intention of covering the 1,100 miles to Karachi in Pakistan, but once again the elements plotted against them, this time in the form of a sandstorm. They were forced to land on a beach some twenty miles west of Bandar Abbas in a 40 m.p.h. crosswind. Crosswind landings are never easy, even in otherwise good conditions, but this one must have been extremely hazardous and not surprisingly the aircraft suffered some damage. The damage was repaired with the use of some angle iron, but the delay meant that they didn't leave Bandar Abbas until the morning of the 24th, arriving at Jask, on the Gulf of Oman at 2.45 p.m. on the same day.

After some further repairs to the aircraft they left Jask on the 3rd March and flew first to Karachi and then on to Delhi, India, arriving on the 11th March.

It was in Karachi that Matthews and Kay met up with the DH 9 crew of Parer and McIntosh. The two teams discussed their experiences and Parer, after hearing of all the difficulties Matthews had experienced, formed the opinion that the Wallaby needed to be landed at high speed or risk losing aileron control.

Since leaving Hounslow on the 21st October 1919 and arriving in Delhi on the 11th March, the Wallaby had actually spent less than 60 hours in the air, with much of the remaining time being spent carrying out repairs, waiting for weather to clear, or incarcerated as prisoners. Matthews and Kay must have felt that the entire world had conspired against them in an effort to prevent them completing their journey within a reasonable time-frame.

Matthews piloted the Wallaby from Delhi to Allahabad in three and a half hours on the 16th March and from Allahabad to Calcutta in four and a half hours on the 17th, where they again met up with Parer and McIntosh in the DH 9, who at the time were busy making some money with advertising stunts and leaflet drops.

After leaving Calcutta on the 24th March there followed another series of relatively short hops, first to Akyab and then

Rangoon. The damaged propeller was restricting their speed
and one wing was slightly damaged landing at Rangoon, delaying their departure until the 30th.

A safe landing was made at Bangkok after an almost six-
hour flight through heavy rain and a strong headwind, and one
would have hoped that some good luck would befall them after all they'd been through, but this was not to be. Kay went
down with a fever and was unable to fly until 7th April, when
they finally managed to get airborne again and head for Singapore. It was necessary first however to land at Singora, on the
Malay Peninsula, to take on more fuel. The weather in the area
had decided to be good for a change, so the next morning they
arrived in Singapore after a flight of just six hours.

Before leaving Singapore for Kalidjati early on the 12th
April, Matthews is reported to have said, "*I shall proceed to Java
today at the same rate of speed and I hope to reach Darwin on
Tuesday 20th April.*"

After further engine problems, they finally took off safely
from Kalidjati on the 16th April but disaster struck! They were
supposed to land at an airfield at Grokgak near Singaradja, the
administrative district of Balibut, but instead, they crashed in
a banana field on the island of Bali. Matthews was unhurt but
Kay had sustained some broken ribs, and worse still, with badly
damaged wings the Wallaby was beyond repair.

It is impossible to imagine the depth of emotion the two
men must have felt, having come so close to completeing their
flight and becoming only the second crew to fly from Britain
to Australia, to have it snatched away from them at the last
minute after overcoming so many trials and tribulations.

The steamer Roggeveen arrived in Australia on the 11th June
with the remains of the Wallaby in its hold and Matthews and
Kay among the passengers. On their return to Melbourne, despite their disappointment, they were full of praise for the way
they had been treated in Thailand and the Indies, insisting that

a letter of thanks be sent to the Commanding Officer of the
Thai Air Force as well as the Governor-Generals of Singaradja
and Batavia.

The steamer Roggeveen arriving in Australia

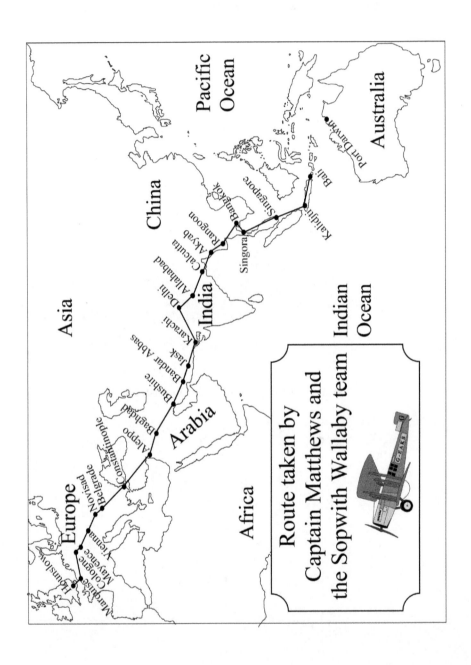

Route taken by
Captain Matthews and
the Sopwith Wallaby team

# Chapter 8

# The DH.9 Team

The Dh.9 team consisted of Lieutenant Raymond John Paul Parer A.F.C. and Lieutenant John Cowie McIntosh A.F.C.

### *Lieutenant Raymond John Paul Parer (1894-1967)*

Lieutenant Raymond Parer

Lieutenant Parer was born in Melbourne, Australia, the second son of nine children born to a Spanish-born caterer, Michael Parer, and his Australian wife Myria (née Carolin). Educated at St. Stanislaus College, New South Wales and Xavier College, Melbourne, he developed an interest in aviation and mechanics at an early age, and served a motor engineering apprenticeship with Broadbribb Brothers in Melbourne.

A motor cycle accident in 1913 resulted in septic poisoning in one leg and for a while it seemed as if he may have needed it amputated, but fortunately this proved unnecessary.

He enlisted in the Australian Flying Corps on 2nd November 1916 as a mechanic, but was later accepted to train as a pilot and given the rank of acting sergeant. From February to May 1917, he trained on Bristol Box Kites at the Central Flying School in Point Cook and was commissioned a second lieutenant on 1 June 1917, after which he was sent to England to complete his training, qualifying as a pilot and being promoted lieutenant on 15th February 1918.

He served as a test and ferry pilot with the Royal Air Force Central Despatch Pool, being twice recommended for the Air Force Cross.

When the Australian Government announced the race, Parer was determined to compete and started looking for backers. His best bet seemed to be with the William Beardmore Aero Company, but even after Ross Smith had started his attempt on the 12th November the company had still not supplied an aircraft. He turned to Captain Matthews, who had the choice of an Alliance or a Sopwith. After opting for the Sopwith, Matthews told Parer he would help him obtain the Alliance, but at that time Parer thought he had an offer from another company and when that fell though, Matthews was already on his way to Australia.

It was only then that he met John Mcintosh and eventually entered the race.

After competing in the race, he formed Parer's Commercial Aviation Service in Melbourne, and on 27th December 1920, he won the first Victorian Aerial Derby in a DH-4, setting a record which stood for a decade. However, his attempt at the first flight to encircle Australia, which he began from Melbourne on 21 October 1921 in an FE2B, ended in disaster when he crashed on take-off at Boulder, Western Australia on 7th February 1922.

Temporarily disillusioned with aviation, he bought a garage on King Island, Tasmania, in the Bass Strait. It would seem that he later regained his interest and became one of the first to fly in New Guinea, one of the world's most hostile environments in which to do so. Gold mining was the only industry to employ aircraft in that part of the world at that time and in 1926 Parer set up the Bulolo Goldfields Aeroplane Service Ltd. and was the first pilot to fly over the Owen Stanley Mountain Range.

In 1934 he took part in the MacRobertson Air Race from England to Australia, this time teamed with Geoffrey Hemsworth and flying a Fairy Fox.

Having returned to New Guinea the impending Japanese invasion in 1942 saw him back in military uniform, this time with the Royal Australian Air Force. Due to his health he was made a reservist, and since he couldn't fly he turned to the sea. He was an engineer aboard the *Melanesia*, which delivered supplies and undertook reconnaissance along New Guinea's northern coastline.

When the war ended, he purchased a ketch and spent some time searching for pearls in the Torres Strait, then from 1949 to 1951, he skippered a barge for the Department of Works around the coast of Papua New Guinea, after which he worked as an engineer on tourist vessels around the Great Barrier Reef. From 1956 to 1958, he returned to Papua New Guinea to work on boats in the oil exploration industry. He spent the last years of his life running two small farms at Mount Nebo, Queensland.

He married Ethel Blanche Jones on 30th December 1941. They later divorced on 8 May 1950 and he was remarried to Mary Patricia Ross, but that marriage also ended in divorce. He died on 4th July 1967 leaving one son.

## *Lieutenant John C. Mcintosh (1892-19210)*

**Lieutenant John McIntosh**

John Cowe McIntosh was born in Scotland in 1892 but having emigrated to Australia he enlisted in the Australian Imperial Force (AIF) at the outbreak of war in 1914.

After serving with the 4th Field Ambulance, Australian Army Medical Corps at Gallipoli and in France he was promoted to Corporal and transferred to the Australian Flying Corps. He was sent to England to undertake flying training at Oxford and was commissioned as a 2nd Lieutenant in April 1919.

After joining Parer in the race to Australia he stayed on and gave joy-rides and flying displays at Pithara, Western Australia.

It was on the 28th March 1921, while flying his single engine De-Havilland aircraft, that the 29 year old McIntosh crashed and was tragically killed. It was the first fatal air crash in Western Australia and a memorial was erected at the site which was then renamed McIntosh Park.

### The Aircraft

The Airco DH.9 also known after 1920 as the de Havilland DH.9 was a British single-engined biplane bomber developed and deployed during the First World War.

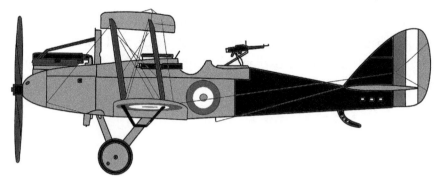

Drawing of an Airco DH 9

With a wingspan of 46 ft. 4 in., and a lengh of 30 ft. 3 in., the DH 9 was a development of Airco's earlier successful aircraft, the DH 4, with which it shared many components. It retained the wings and tailplane of the DH 4, although it had a modified fuselage that moved the pilot closer to the observer, and further away from the engine and fuel tank; and a BHP Galloway *Adriatic* engine, which promised increased performance. The Royal Flying Corps ordered the aircraft in large numbers, but after entering service the DH.9's performance was found to be less than expected.

The engine proved unable to reliably deliver its expected power, having been de-rated to 230 hp (186 kW) in order to improve its reliability. This deficit had a drastic effect on the aircraft's performance, especially at high altitude, and resulted in it being inferior to that of the DH.4 it was supposed to replace. This shortfall in the performance was blamed for the heavy losses they suffered over the Western Front.

At the end of the war the redesigned DH 9A was fitted with a more powerful and reliable American Liberty L-12 engine which rectified the shortcomings of the original DH.9 model and gave it a maximum speed of 123 mph. This new model was produced in the thousands even though production was curtailed by the signing of the Armistice that had ended the First

World War. Belgium and Spain also produced the type, the latter producing hundreds equipped with a 300 hp Hispano-Suiza engine and some of those were still in service as late as 1940.


## The Flight


Exactly why Ray Parer was so excited about the prospect of teaming up with McIntosh, is unclear, but the two men seemed to hit it off straight away, despite that fact that McIntosh had little experience, having been transferred from the infantry to the R.A.F. only a short time before the Armistice, had made few flights, and knew little of navigation.

The two men pooled their resources and set aside the £100 entry fee for the race. They spent weeks looking for a suitable plane and their hopes of entering the race were dwindling when they met an A.I.F. officer who was returning from Scotland. Lieutenant G. H. Thornton told them about a Scottish distiller and millionaire called Peter Dawson, who just might agree to back them.

After meeting Parer and learning of his experience Dawson handed McIntosh a cheque enabling them to purchase an old Airco DH.9 G-EAQM, (formerly the RAF's F1278) which had been bought from the Aircraft Disposal Company as unwanted war surplus.

Just as the pair were about to leave on their adventurous undertaking, news reached them of the arrival of Ross Smith and the Vickers Vimy in Darwin and the Air Ministry returned Parer and McIntosh's deposit.

The venture, which had taken so long to put together, seemed dashed at the last moment, but when news of the latest events reached Peter Dawson, he immediately sent a message saying, "*Carry on and good luck to you.*" He also guaranteed to cover payment of any "in transit" expenditure.

All they needed now was permission to continue from the Australian Defence Department. Determined to wait no longer, the pair set off immediately for Hounslow, but darkness forced them to land in a field between Waddon and Hounslow and this in turn resulted in the two pilots being apprehended by the local police.

The next day, having satisfied the police department of their legitimacy and enlisting the help of some locals, a makeshift runway was established by the removal of three fences. The runway however proved too short after the first attempt, so the aircraft was made lighter, Parer taking off solo and McIntosh making his way to Hounslow by train.

Embarrassment was to follow on account of Parer being unable to locate Hounslow and having to return to Wadden and make another attempt. Although they tried to keep Parer's navigational error a secret, news leaked out, and it was whispered in some quarters, "how is he going to find Australia, if he can't locate Hounslow?"

Two telegrams had arrived at Hounslow but Parer, possibly suspecting bad news from the Australian Defence Department, didn't view the contents, preferring to take a chance and leave for Australia.

So eventually, on the 8th January 1920 the pair took off at 10.40a.m. bound for Paris. They crossed the channel at 5.000 feet and were within sight of Boulogne before conditions deteriorated and they encountered cloud. Unable to fly above the cloud, Parer descended to 600 feet but visibility was still poor, so he took the decision to land in the first suitable field, and this resulted in a buckled right wheel.

Learning from locals that they had landed at Conteville and that the rail line to Paris was only 14 miles distant, Parer hitchhiked his way on various carts and managed to get on a train to Paris.

Once he arrived in Paris, he lost little time in locating Le Bourget airfield and hangers belonging to Airco Channel Services. The manager there agreed , after some persuasion, to let Parer have a wheel of approximately the right size. It could not have been the easiest of tasks to trundle the wheel back to Paris and then get it on a train back to the field where McIntosh was waiting anxiously. The undercarriage had also been damaged in the landing but while Parer had been off in search of a replacement wheel, McIntosh had secured the help of a local blacksmith and between them they had carried out repairs. They must have breathed a big sigh of relief when the wheel was finally fitted.

Bad weather prevented their departure until the 14th January when they flew to Le Bourget, where Parer had obtained the wheel, and as the weather was bad the two men did the touristy thing and visited the Folies Bergères in Paris. The two men in their Australian uniforms and holstered Colt revolvers were apparently the toast of the town and a big hit with the ladies.

On the 17th January they took off for Lyons which they reached after some searching. The intention had been to follow the rivers between the two cities but flooding had made this difficult. Nevertheless they landed at Lyons without incident.

It was the 19th January when they once again took to the air, this time with McIntosh at the controls, and against the advice of local weather officials who had urged delaying until conditions improved. Visibility was indeed bad but they managed to spot a railway line leading to Marseilles and were able to land at St Raphael where there was a French flying base.

After showing their Air Ministry documents to the commanding officer of the base, he was happy to allocate a mechanic to help with repairs that included stopping an oil leak and repairing a split exhaust pipe.

After taking the opportunity for a much needed rest they were in the air again on the 22nd January, this time heading for Pisa. After a while in the air Parer noticed that the oil pressure had dropped drastically. Priority was to make it to land and get the aircraft down before the engine seized up. The nearest airfield was Sarzana in Italy that they estimated to be about 100 miles further on. Fearful that the engine could seize at any minute Parer flew on and after sighting the airfield decided to fly straight in and land without doing the usual circuit and approach. One can only imagine the relief the pair must have felt when Parer was finally able to swich the engine off.

After confirming that the oil tank was almost empty, the DH.9 was wheeled into a vacant hanger and the two weary pilots walked the four miles into the village of Sarzana and booked into a boarding house for the night. McIntosh, having consumed too much of the local wine, apparently had nightmares and awoke the next morning on the floor beside his bed.

Although McIntosh had suffered from nightmares during the night, he could have had no inkling of the real nightmare that they would both face later that same day.

Employing the help of a couple of local boys to pull a small cart back to the airfield with the newly acquired cans of oil on board, they lost no time in refilling the oil tank and checking for leaks. When the engine was running however, they detected a misfire. Parer thought it would probably clear itself when in flight, as carburettors in those days often did, and made the decision to take off anyway. However, even after they had reached a height of some 3.000 feet the engine was still misfiring.

It was then with some horror that Parer spotted petrol gushing from the engine, and although he quickly shut off the throttle he was not fast enough, and a sheet of flame followed as the hot exhaust pipes ignited the fuel. The flames were reaching all the way back from the engine to Parer's elbows.

Both aircraft and crew were now in real trouble as the flames quickly began to scorch the plywood fuselage. It was fortunate however, both that they had some height to play with and that Parer was an experienced pilot who kept a clear head in a crisis. Knowing that he had to get the aircraft on the ground as quickly as possible as well as protect it from the fire, he immediately banked the aircraft, and this, without the use of any rudder, caused the aircraft to sideslip away from the flames at a 90-degree angle. He held the aircraft in the sideslip as long as he dare, and the gods must have decided, in the whimsical way they sometimes do, to reward his quick thinking, for when they were no more than 1,000 feet from the ground, the fire had been blown out by the air rushing past the fuselage and miraculously, almost directly below them was the abandoned aerodrome of Forte di Marmi. Still having to keep a cool head and using all his piloting skills, Parer managed to land safely.

On examination the fuselage of the aircraft was found to be badly scorched but still structurally sound. The cause of the trouble was found to be no more than a bent carburettor needle and this was quickly repaired.

Taking to the air again they decided to fly straight to Rome rather than stopping at Pisa. They reached Rome safely, but funds had just about run out, the two men having left Hounslow with less than £50.00 between them. It was time to see if Peter Dawson was as good as his word, and a cable requesting funds was immediately sent to Scotland. How the two must have felt checking in to the Hotel Royal in the state they must have been in we don't know, neither man carried luggage with them, it was an unnecessary weight in the aircraft, but at least they could now wash and shave.

Shortly after they had arrived in Rome a Vickers Vimy also landed. Commanded by a Captain Cockerill it was on its way to Cairo to compete in a flight from Cairo to Capetown and the two crews are reputed to have had breakfast together the next morning.

Peter Dawson was indeed as good as his word and all bills were paid, allowing the two to set off again on the 2nd February, bound for Naples.

Let's face it, the two men were adventurers and one of them, McIntosh, a keen photographer, so to view the smoking crater of Mount Vesuvius from the air was always going to be an irresistible draw. As they flew over the crater, Parer recalls that it felt as if the aircraft had been struck a physical blow and the engine briefly cut out as the DH.9 plunged downwards. Luckily the engine restarted and choking from sulphur fumes they managed to regain control and land at Naples. Both men fell to the ground on exiting the plane, bruised, exhausted and still choking on fumes, but at least still alive.

Aware that Italy was in an unstable political situation with shortages of both money and goods, Parer and McIntosh were keen to leave as soon as they could. Despite being in need of some time to recover from their recent ordeals, they left Naples on the 3rd February, bound for Taranto.

To reach their destination it was necessary to fly over the Apennines Mountain. At 7,000 feet they hit cloud so Parer had no option other than to gain height to get above it, eventually reaching 14,000 feet. Without oxygen at that height for some three hours and in their poor physical condition they could make it no further than St. Euphemia near Stromboli.

At St. Euphemia their run of bad luck continued when they discovered that the nearest supply of petrol was back in Naples, and due to railway regulations it couldn't be transported by train. Eventually, thanks to intervention by the British Consul authorities, the regulations were overcome but the 200-litre drum of petrol had to be hand rolled the 5 miles from the railway station to the airfield.

The DH.9 and its now slightly more rested crew eventually made it to Taranto dirigible station on the 7<sup>th</sup> February and the Italian airmen there made them more than welcome. They stayed in Taranto for five days, time to service the aircraft and catch up on some sleep.

Leaving Taranto on the 12<sup>th</sup> February they once again had engine problems and headed for the nearest airfield at Brindisi. At Brindisi they found that the problem had been with the fuel-pump and that was quickly repaired. They were also surprised to once again meet up with Captain Cockerill and his Vickers Vimy with whom they had previously shared breakfast in Rome.

The next day they set off for Athens, but as planned, they first flew to Corfu where they dropped a wreath in St, Georges Bay where Captain Howell and Lieutenant Fraser lost their lives. They later landed safely at Goode Aerodrome near Athens, where they stayed for five days.

AUSTRALIAN WAR MEMORIAL                                    P00281.005

The DH 9 at the aerodrme near Athens

Although relations between Greece and Britain were not at their best at this time, de Haviland were trying to sell aircraft to the Greek Government. Having the DH 9 there was a God-send for the de Haviland representative and Parer and McIntosh agreed to do some demonstration flights while they were there.

After Athens the next stop was Suda Bay on Crete and they landed there on 18th February. This was where the Wilkins' Blackburn Kangaroo had ended its journey and Parer and McIntosh found Lt Potts, from the Kangaroo's crew, stuck on the island looking after his aeroplane. Despite Potts' pleas to stay longer, the DH 9 crew left Crete for Egypt two days later.

There was no airfield at Mersah Matruh, their destination in Egypt, so they landed the DH 9 on a hard beach, completing the first crossing of the Mediterranean Sea by a single engined aircraft. On the approach to Mersah Matruh the engine had once again been misfiring and causing to lose them height, so much so that in the end, both airmen had inflated their life belts in preparation for a ditching at sea, that thankfully was avoided.

As it turned out they had arrived just in the nick of time because the ship that had been sent to remove their supplies, including fuel, had just arrived. Had they arrived just one day later, their precious fuel would have been on its way home.

The next day they left for and landed at Cairo, where they were less than welcome. The aerodrome was full of aircraft being prepared to compete in the Cairo to Cape Town flight, so they were asked to please move on to Heliopolis. This was done, and the DH 9 received a much needed overhaul from the RAF before flying on to Baghdad on 26th February.

The intention had been to fly direct to Baghdad but they were informed that much of the territory was occupied by hostile Arabs and they were advised to return to London. The airmen were determined to press on however. They were given fresh maps covering the area and advised to go first to Ramleh in Palestine and there to request an escort from an R.A.F. aircraft well into the desert where they would both land and the DH 9 could be re-fuelled with petrol from a bulk supply carried on the R.A.F. Handley-Page plane. The R.A.F. plane would then return to Cairo and the DH 9 would push on to Baghdad.

When it became clear that Parer and McIntosh could not be dissuaded from continuing, the commanding officer made sure that they were well supplied for the journey with bully beef, brandy, biscuits, water and, just in case, a supply of hand-grenades!

As it turned out the R.A.F. was unable to supply an aircraft so they had to leave Ramleh without the hoped-for escort.

After some flying time, the engine began to play up, which necessitated a landing in the desert for some fairly quick attention before getting back into the air. Unfortunately, the time on the ground meant that Baghdad couldn't be reached in daylight, and another desert landing was necessary.

The desert night was cold and, after burning what bushes were available in an effort to generate some heat, the men had to sleep in the aeroplane. Dawn brought both light and a number of unfriendly, but fortunately unarmed, Arabs to the DH 9.

Hastily climbing aboard, it seemed that the arrival of the Arabs might hinder the take off so McIntosh threw one of the grenades as a warning. The grenade put off the advance of the unwelcome visitors long enough for the pair to get airborne.

Thirty minutes flying brought the men to Baghdad on 28th February, where they arrived to find that they were unexpected, as no signal advising of their forthcoming arrival had been received. The aircraft was in need of attention, including a replacement propeller. The old propeller and some additional spares were sent on to Karachi by boat.

They departed for Basra on 2nd March and there, Parer and McIntosh crossed paths with aircraft competing in the Rome-Tokyo Race. After a brief stay in Basra, the airmen headed for for Bushire on the Persian Gulf and then on to Bandar Abbas in Persia on 5th March, only to encounter a fierce dust storm on the way.

These dust storms were commonplace and Parer and McIntosh were not the only team to encounter one. At first, they climbed to a height of over 8,000 feet hoping to get above the storm but the red sand got into their mouths, ears and noses, even at that height, so Parer, afraid that the sand might clog the engine air intakes or foul the carburettor, decided it would be saver to fly over water rather than land and headed out to sea.

It was with immense relief that the airmen eventually made it through the storm despite being covered in sand and thrown about like dice in a cup. Heading back towards land they were happy to sight Bandar Abbas where they landed safely and spent the night as guests of the British Consul.

More dust storms were encountered the following day, as the machine flew to Chah Bahar, in Persia, and then on to Karachi the next day, where the crew met Matthews and Kay in their Sopwith Wallaby.

**Onlookers at Char Bahar**

Leaving Karachi on the 8th March Parer and McIntosh encountered bad turbulence and were buffeted about for several hours. Landing at Nasirabad for fuel they made the decision to stay over for the night. In the RAF mess that night they were warned about flying over the State of Jaipur, (an independent state at the time) because if they had to land there, they would not be welcome. The Rajah had six wives and required complete privacy for his harem. A railway that had been built across his land had been diverted to the very corner of it on his insistence.

Jaipur was nevertheless on the airmen's intended route and McIntosh delighted in taking pictures of the Rajah's palace as they passed by. On landing at Delhi they were pleased to meet up with Matthews again who was delayed there with a damaged propeller.

The reception they received at Delhi from the Commanding Officer was somewhat less warm than the airmen had expected, so the pair decided to leave the next day, to the obvious disappointment of Matthews.

Their next stop was Allahabad to refuel. The following morning, the 12$^{th}$ March they set off for Calcutta. Both men were tired and run down and the aircraft was beginning to act up again. They would undoubtedly have stayed over at Delhi if their reception had been warmer, but the decision had been made.

There was no reason for them to suppose that things would get any easier and indeed, not long after leaving Delhi they encountered some of the worst weather they had experienced so far, this time in the form of thunder and lightning storms.

With nowhere safe to near by they had no option other than to press on, trying as best they could to avoid the worst of the storms. Sometimes having to fly blind, Parer lost sight of the river he had been following. Fortunately they soon spotted a railway line and began following that, only to have it disappear in thick forest. Consulting maps, they managed to identify a landmark that happily placed them no more than two hours flying time from Calcutta.

They landed at Calcutta at 1.30 p.m. and were greeted by Officials from the Handley Page Company, who arranged to have the DH 9 undergo a badly needed overhaul. The main problem facing Parer and McIntosh at this point however was a distinct lack of funds, as they were down to only 6 shillings between them. In an effort to become financially viable again, the airmen embarked on a number of fund-raising projects, including leaflet drops and aerobatic displays. Despite the fact they were building up their funds, Parer had decided to carry out the necessary repairs to the DH 9 himself to save money.

One night at dinner the pair met an ex-Indian Army Major. Major Cairncross introduced himself and said that he was writing a book on the England to Calcutta stage of the race and he offered them some kind of beneficial financial arrangement.

Good news and bad news followed. Matthews arrived with the news that Parer and McIntosh had been accused of leaving

Delhi without paying for their fuel, an oversight on McIntosh's part that caused them some embarrassment. Following a display of aerobatics at a race meeting, the club involved presented the pair with a gratefully received cheque for £400.

The leaflet drops also proved very lucrative if a bit controversial in some quarters. Police were concerned that the leaflets could disturb cattle or frighten horses. At one point, Lipton Tea provided Parer and McIntosh with one thousand leaflets promising a one-pound bag of tea to all finders but it seemed that another printer had also prepared a supply of the leaflets that he sold off at a reasonable price, so Lipton had to supply far more tea than they had expected.

With the money in their coffers increasing nicely they received the further good news that Peter Dawson had established a line of credit for them, so their debts could all be paid off, and for the time being at least they were free of financial restraints.

They left Calcutta for Akyab, Burma, on 1st April. With both crew and machine now in good order the journey was for once uneventful, which was just as well, as the terrain over which they flew alternated between dense forest and paddy-fields, either one of which could have proved fatal in the event of a forced landing.

The first day in Burma passed well, but on the 2nd April the planned flight from Akyab to Rangoon was to follow the coast as far as Sandoway when they would cross the mountains to the Irrawaddy River that would lead them to Rangoon. This involved them flying over mountains and jungle that were said to be inhabited by unfriendly natives who were rumoured to indulge in the odd bit of cannibalism.

With this knowledge in mind, the airmen must have been extremely alarmed when the carburettor choked off the fuel supply to the engine, forcing the aeroplane to land on a small island in the Irrawaddy River.

When the aircraft rolled to a stop on the bank of the island, Parer was out of the cockpit, had the cowling off and was attending to the engine in moments. Nevertheless, as they worked on the engine, hundreds of Burmese appeared on the banks of the river, eager to see just what was happening with this strange thing that had dropped from the sky.

After a while, some of the more adventurous natives swam to the island and crowded around the aeroplane, until McIntosh dispersed them with a flare from a Very pistol.

When the repairs to the engine were completed, their problems were by no means over. Somehow, they had to get back in the air. By now there were far fewer natives and those that remained showed no signs of hostility, only curiosity, so by a mixture of gesture and sign language, Parer and McIntosh persuaded some of the locals to carry the aeroplane across the river to the opposite bank.

The airmen must have had to pinch themselves to be sure they weren't dreaming as they watched their precious DH 9 carried across a river on the shoulders of a small army of men wading more than waist deep. After the aircraft was safely on the bank they also manage to somehow convey to their new-found ground-crew, that they needed a runway to be cleared.

With mounting enthusiasum now, reinforcements were summoned and a rudimentary runway was hacked out with the help of hundreds of now willing volunteers armed with machetes.

When the runway was finished there were still some hours of daylight to come, so the two airmen boarded the DH 9 and, probably with fingers crossed, managed to take off. Two hours later they landed at Rangoon with an enormous sigh of relief that they had ended the day in Rangoon, rather than the dreaded cooking pot they had half expected.

At Rangoon, their reception was a little frosty as the aeroplane was late, and the airmen were informed in no uncertain terms that they had kept everyone waiting for hours.

Parer and McIntosh stayed in Rangoon for a few days, which was enough time for them both to receive proposals of marriage from an extremely wealthy Chinese businessman who was keen to have his daughters marry European officers. It must have been a tempting offer, as not only were the ladies in question considered quite beautiful, there was also a gratuity of thirty thousand rupees for each. This, with the backing of a wealthy father-in-law would have been enough to see the two airmen set up a small airline between them. However, the offers were politely declined and they left for Victoria Point on the 4th April.

The 100 mile wide Gulf of Martaban now lay before them and they soon regretted not taking the time in Rangoon to overhaul the engine, as half way across the Gulf it began to misfire and vibrate. Things quickly got worse as a hole developed in an exhaust pipe causing flame to leap down the right-hand side of the cockpit. Parer, who had been watching the engine closely, saw that fuel had begun to leak from the gravity tank and that three of the engine cylinders appeared to be loose. After a while, the engine simply stopped, and at 4000 feet, and in thick cloud, the DH 9 began to glide. McIntosh then started to blow up the tyre inner tubes that were carried as elementary life vests, while Parer prepared for a ditching. At this point, whether from divine intervention or just good luck, the engine decided to splutter back into life and the aircraft staggered towards the coastal town of Moulmein, where the racecourse was the designated landing ground.

As Parer approached, he could see that most of the racecourse was covered with people (including the Frenchman Poulet) who were out to have a look at the aeroplane and the intrepid airmen. The police tried their best to clear a landing path, but without a great deal of success. Parer even considered firing some shots from his revolver to disperse the crowd, but fearing it would cause panic and do more harm than good, he decided against it.

In the end, the only alternative to crashing into hundreds of people, was for Parer to crash land in an area reasonably devoid of people and, fortunately for those involved, he managed to succeed in that endeavour with no one being injured. The same could not be said for the DH 9 however.

On inspection it was revealed that the propeller was broken, the radiator crushed, the fuel tanks damaged, and the undercarriage wrecked. Parer was furious and angrily pushed away people who had come to congratdulate them, convinced that their adventure was over.

The damaged DH 9 at Moulmein

In 1920 aeroplane parts were somewhat thin on the ground in Asia, and the situation looked pretty grim. Two Italian mechanics were brought from Calcutta, and attended to much of the work, but the propeller and radiator were the main problems. However in an inspired piece of improvisation, two Overland car radiators were bolted together to replace the aeroplane's damaged one.

A propeller was found in Calcutta, but it turned out to be too heavy for the DH 9 and Parer doubted whether it would operate satisfactorily. He also doubted that the racecourse was long enough for the DH 9 to take off fully loaded.

Sixty miles away from the racecourse, there was a large stretch of beach at Amherst, so it was decided that McIntosh should transport most of the fuel and other heavy bits and pieces there by road and that Parer would take off using the main road as a runway and the aircraft as lightly loaded as possible.

The flight to Amherst and the beach landing went according to plan and the plane was filled with fuel. The take-off was also achieved, although with an ill-matched propeller, they were not able to gain much height until they had used some of the fuel and lightened the aircraft. Nevertheless, after five hours in the air they landed at Victoria Point on the 27th May.

The day our intrepid pair left Victoria Point, the 28th May, lots of locals turned out dressed in their best clothes to see them off and even presented them with a farewell present of a Siamese cat in a basket. It would seem however that the cat was not an aviation enthusiast and escaped from the basket at the first oppertunity. After a brief effort to avoid recapture by McIntosh, it leapt out of the aircraft as it started its take-off run and was last seen being chased by the surrounding crowd, and probably wondering what it had done to receive such punishment.

After leaving Victoria Point things went fairly smoothly for a while, that is, until the engine seized after the oil pressure dropped when the aeroplane was approaching Penang on 28th

May. The DH 9 came down on a polo field at Georgetown, much to the chagrin of the polo players who were using it at the time, but once again nobody was injured.

The aircraft was moved to the side of the field and a block and tackle were used to lift the engine out of its housing for examination. It was the 16<sup>th</sup> June before all the repairs to the seized engine were completed and it was once again able to be reunited with the airframe. Engine problems resolved, there was now the question of a suitable runway, the polo field being far too short.

The aircraft was towed through the streets to a racecourse where the straight was 600 yards long, but even so, officials at the course needed a great deal of persuading, and who knows, perhaps a little financial incentive to agree to the cutting down of two trees.

After taking off for Singapore and only a few miles out from Penang an exhaust pipe fractured. Parer elected to return, and landed at a rubber estate, only to have the tailskid break on landing. After repairs, the men left again and arrived in Singapore the next day, landing at yet another racecourse.

In Singapore again, Mr Charles Wearne an Australian businessman, allowed them the use of his auto workshop to carry out repairs, and also cabled his agent in Djakarta for a replacement propeller and radiator. By the time the replacement parts arrived the aircraft had been completely repainted and once more looked as if it could cope with the task ahead of it. The new propeller fitted perfectly but the radiator proved unsuitable and they had to make do with the makeshift one they had. The aircraft fuselage had been sporting an advert for the Shell Company and an enterprising Parer managed to negotiate free fuel from them for the remainder of the flight. The bad news was that there would be no warship stationed between Timor and Darwin so if the DH 9 came down in the sea there would be no one standing by to rescue the fliers. Parer and McIntosh were undaunted however, perhaps because they had survived so much already and perhaps in part because the DH 9, now with its new propeller and paint job, inspired renewed confidence.

It was the 20th July when they took off for Muntok but Parer had underestimated the severity of the weather and after being tossed about by a strong headwind for almost three hours without making any great headway they returned to Singapore and stayed another night. The winds had abated by the following morning and they made it to Muntok, then in the Dutch East Indies, in relative ease.

At this point the airmen considered flying to Broome in Western Australia, rather than direct to Darwin, as that route would take them over islands every 200 miles, but the idea was abandoned and they proceeded to Kalidjati.

A forced landing in a river bed due to magneto problems when flying from Kalidjati to Samarang on 23rd July turned out to be the last such landing on the journey, but the men's troubles were by no means over.

At Sourabana on 24th July the aeroplane ran into a ditch after landing, crushing the undercarriage and breaking the propeller. Fortunately, the Dutch authorities were able to assist with both repairs and spare parts – including yet another replacement propeller, and the DH 9 was able to depart for Bima in West Timor on 30th July. After Bima, the next flight was to Atamboea – the last stop before Darwin!

At Atamboea, time was spent preparing for the long over water flight to Darwin, including fashioning a raft from fuel tanks and bamboo, with a (hopefully) shark-proof wire mesh floor. The raft was secured under the aeroplane, with the idea of using the fuel from the external tanks first, so that the empty tanks would float in the event of a ditching. The attached raft probably did very little for the aerodynamics of the

DH 9, but would have been very useful if needed. Finally, on 2 August, G-EAQM left Timor for Darwin.

The aeroplane wouldn't climb very well with the additional load and drag caused by the raft, so the flight across the Timor Sea took some six hours, which was far longer than expected, and the crew were understandably very relieved when Bathurst Island finally came into sight. Forty five minutes after passing over the island, the DH 9 finally touched down in Darwin, and then came to a stop as its fuel supply was finally exhausted.

Incredibly, a bottle of whisky had survived the entire journey and its various mishaps, and was presented to Prime Minister Hughes.

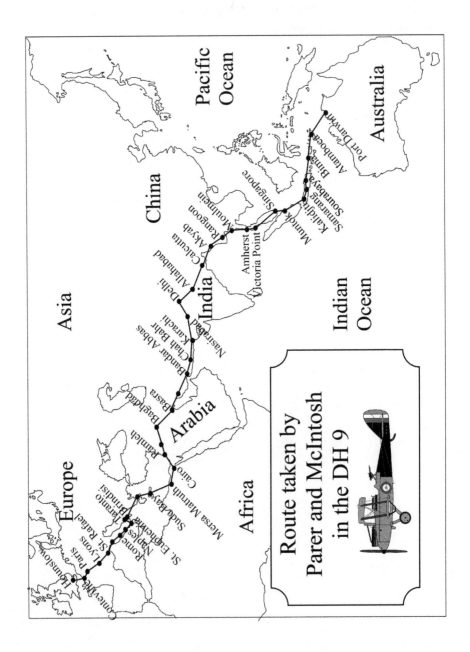

Route taken by Parer and McIntosh in the DH 9

# Chapter 9

# The Vickers Vimy Team

*Captain Sir Ross Macpherson Smith*

Ross Macpherson Smith (1892-1922)

Ross Macpherson Smith was born on the 4th December 1892 in Semaphore in South Australia, the second son of Scottish-born Andrew Bell Smith and Mrs Jessie Smith nee Macpherson.

He was educated at Queen's School, North Adelaide where he was captain of the school cricket team and Warriston School, Moffat, Scotland, his father's birthplace.

On returning to Australia, Ross joined the Australian

Mounted Cadets and was selected in 1910 to tour Britain and the United States of America as a South Australian representative. He then joined the 10th Australian Regiment, the Adelaide Rifles.

Before the outbreak of war in 1914 Ross was employed as a warehouseman in Adelaide for G. P. Harris Scarfe & Co. When hostilities began in 1914 he enlisted as a private in the 3rd Light Horse Regiment, Australian Imperial Force, and on 1st October was promoted to sergeant. He embarked for Egypt on 22nd October and landed on Gallipoli on 13th May 1915. On 11th August he attained the rank of regimental sergeant major and was commissioned second lieutenant on 5th September.

Invalided to England in October, he was promoted lieutenant on 1st March 1916 and three weeks later embarked for Egypt to re-join his old regiment. With the 1st Light Horse Brigade, 1st Machine-Gun Squadron, his principal action occurred during the battle of Romani on 4th August 1916. In July 1917 he responded to a call for volunteers to join the Australian Flying Corps, and was eccepted on 4th August.

Qualifying as an observer in December 1916, and later as a pilot, he served mainly with No.1 Squadron, Australian Flying Corps (No. 67 Squadron R.F.C.), a general purpose squadron flying a variety of aircraft in defence of the Suez Canal zone. In January 1918 it was re-equipped with the Bristol Fighter and designated as a fighter squadron. As such the squadron was an important element of General (Lord) Allenby's 1918 offensive and took part in the overwhelming air attacks on the Turkish armies in the Wadi Fara. For a while Ross was assigned as one of the personal pilots for Thomas Edward Lawrence, known better as Lawrence of Arabia

By the end of the war Ross had twice been decorated with the Military Cross and three times with the Distinguished Flying Cross, and he was later to add the Air Force Cross for non-operational flying. The first Military Cross was awarded on the

11<sup>th</sup> May 1917 while Ross, still an observer, landed in the face of the enemy to rescue a fellow officer who had been brought down. Ross held the enemy back with his revolver while his pilot helped the stricken officer. He was awarded a bar to his Military Cross on the 26<sup>th</sup> March 1918 for carrying out both dangerous photographic missions and a daring bombing raid at low level on a bridgehead.

On the 8<sup>th</sup> February 1918 he, along with Lieutenant A. Kirk, D.F.C., was awarded the Distinguished Flying Cross and bar for carrying out several low level attacks, as well as bringing down two enemy machines and showing great initiative and gallantry. He received a second bar for forcing down an enemy plane, and on seeing it land intact, landed beside it, and while his observer covered the enemy officers, set light to it and completely destroyed it.

By the end of the war Ross had acquired considerable experience flying the twin-engined Handley Page 0/400 bomber which he had flown, not only on bombing operations in Palestine but also on long photographic flights. As a result of his experience, he was selected to co-pilot the aircraft in a pioneer flight from Cairo to Calcutta, leaving Cairo on 29th November 1918 and arriving in Calcutta on 10th December.

After their success in the 1919 flight to Australia, Ross and his brother Keith's next proposal was to fly round the world in a Vickers Viking amphibian, but this ended in disaster. Both brothers travelled to England to prepare for the trip and on 13th April 1922, while Ross and his long-serving crew member Bennett were test-flying the aircraft at Weybridge near London, when it spun into the ground from 1000 feet, killing them both. The tragedy was witnessed by brother Keith who had arrived late for the test flight.

Ross had not flown at all for many months and had never flown this type of aircraft. The investigating committee concluded that the accident had been the result of pilot error.

The flight was abandoned and the bodies of Sir Ross Smith and Lieutenant Bennett were brought home to Australia and after a state funeral Smith was buried in Adelaide on 15th June.

During his life, apart from his Military Cross with bar and the Distinguished Flying Cross with two bars, Ross had also been awarded the Air Force Cross, The Order of El Nahda, (awarded by the King of Hejaz for conspicuous gallantry) and he was made a Knight Commander of the British Empire for the flight from England to Australia.

## *Lieutenant Keith Macpherson Smith*

Keith Macpherson Smith (1890- 1955)

Sir Keith Macpherson Smith was born on 20th December 1890 in Adelaide, making him two years younger than his brother Ross.

Although Keith's early career differed from his brother's, they both became involved in aviation within weeks of each other.

Employed by Elder Smith & Co. in Adelaide on the outbreak of war, Keith was rejected for service with the A.I.F. on medical grounds. After undergoing medical treatment, he paid for his own passage to England to enlist in the Royal Flying Corps and was accepted in July 1917 into the Officer Cadet Wing. He was posted in November of that year to No. 58 Squadron, a newly formed bomber unit which left for France in January 1918.

Keith, however, was destined not to see active service. On 24th February 1918 he was posted to No. 75 Squadron, a home-defence formation, as a gunnery instructor. On 1st April that year he was promoted lieutenant and spent the rest of the war in Britain with training establishments. He was placed on the unemployed list, R.A.F., on 5th November 1919.

A little while after witnessing his brother's tragic death during a test flight of a Vickers Vimy at Weybridge, near London on 13th April 1922, Sir Keith Smith was appointed Australian agent for Vickers and retained the connection with this British company until his death.

Between the wars it seems that Vickers took little interest in the small Australian market and despite Smith's efforts, no aircraft were sold until the arrival of the Viscount in 1954. One promising venture that was strongly supported by Smith in the early 1920s, was to employ Vickers-built airships on Imperial air routes. After all a British airship had successfully crossed the Atlantic in July 1919, but projects failed to materialize. After a general election the British government changed and so did policy, especially after the airship which had crossed the Atlantic, the R34, was destroyed in a sudden and violent storm.

Keith remained, however, possibly the leading Australian spokesman on aviation matters and travelled extensively on Vickers' behalf. He held firmly to the view that Imperial co-operation was vital in aviation and looked for complete standardization of British and Australian equipment. In the end it was British indifference to the threat posed by the rapidly improving American aircraft industry that was to eventually defeat this aspiration.

He went on to become, vice-president of British Commonwealth Pacific Airlines, a director of Qantas and Tasman Airways and by the end of his career was in control of the many Australian-based Vickers companies.

In World War II he was vice-chairman of the Royal Australian Air Force Recruiting Drive Committee and strongly supported the idea of an Empire air force.

In 1924 Keith had married Anita Crawford of Adelaide who survived him when he died of cancer in Sydney on 19th December 1955. He had no children but left an estate valued at £33,723. Included in his will was a bequest of £100 to W. H. Shiers, the sole remaining crew member of the England-Australia flight. The Vickers Vimy flown on that occasion is displayed at Adelaide airport. Sir Keith Smith was buried near his brother, father and mother in the North Road Anglican cemetery, Adelaide.

### Sergeant Walter Henry (Wally) Shiers

Walter Henry Shiers (1889-1968)

Walter Henry Shiers, was born on 17th May 1889 at Norwood, Adelaide, son of William Thomas Shiers, a plasterer, and his wife Annie, née Haire. He came from a family of twelve and attended Richmond Public School, Keswick, until 1902 when he began work with a market gardener and learned the rudiments of pump and motor maintenance.

After the death of his mother in 1904 he moved in to live with his eldest brother at Broken Hill, New South Wales, and worked at the Broken Hill North Mine until December 1912.

In 1913 he began an electrical contracting business at Leeton where he worked until 1915 although it is uncertain whether he was ever actually indentured in the trade.

Having enlisted as a trooper in the 1st Light Horse Regiment, Australian Imperial Force, on 9 April 1915, Shiers embarked for Egypt in June. In July 1916 he was transferred to No.67 (Australian) Squadron, Royal Flying Corps, which later became No.1 Squadron, Australian Flying Corps, and he was promoted 1st class air mechanic in November 1917.

Shiers first came to prominence as an engineer by participating on the first flight from Cairo to Calcutta in November-December 1918, a year before the England to Australia flight.

He was promoted sergeant from 10th December 1919, the date of the Smiths' arrival in Darwin, and on his discharge in 1920 he was granted the honorary rank of lieutenant, A.I.F. as well as being awarded the Air Force Medal and a Bar for his part in the two flights. His medals are held by the Art Gallery of South Australia.

Shiers married Helena Lydia Alford at Bellevue Hill, Sydney, on 17th February 1920, but the union produced no children. Early in the 1920s he operated a garage at Bondi Junction and, following a visit to England in 1922 with the Smith brothers (when Sir Ross died in a plane crash), he worked for various aviation companies at Mascot.

In 1925 he began barnstorming with Dave Smith, a Sydney pilot who owned a Ryan monoplane, and after obtaining his pilot's licence (No.408) on 20th November 1929, he planned to fly to England with Smith. They left Sydney on 30th March 1930 but after a forced landing in the Ord River area of Western Australia and a crash landing in Siam (Thailand) the flight was abandoned.

On his return to Australia, Shiers joined New England Airways, which later became Airlines of Australia for which he was chief engineer until 1939. For the next six years he was in charge of the textiles branch of the Light Aircraft Co. which manufactured parachutes for the defence forces.

He received a war pension for the injuries he received in World War I and from 1945 while living at Dover Heights, Sydney his health deteriorated.

At the dedication of the memorial of the first England-Australia flight at Adelaide airport in April 1958 Shiers, the only surviving crew member, was present. He is depicted in the sculpture of the four aviators by John Dowie.

**Sculpture by John Dowie at Adelaide Airport**

From 1965 he lived in Adelaide where he died of heart disease on 2nd June 1968; he was buried in Centennial Park cemetery. Friends and acquaintances remember Wally Shiers as a short nuggetty man of great character who had a strong will and abrupt manner, although generous to a fault.

## James Mallett (Jim) Bennett (1894-1922)

James Mallett (Jim) Bennett
(1894-1922)

James Mallett Bennett airman and mechanic, was born on 14 January 1894 at St Kilda, Victoria, son of James Thomas Bennett and his wife Henrietta Augusta, née McKendrick.

After he finished school James trained as a motor mechanic and in 1912 he joined the militia and served for three years with the 49th Battalion.

He enlisted in the Australian Imperial Force on 14th July 1915 and, on the formation of the Australian Flying Corps early next year, was posted to 'C' Flight, No. 1 Squadron, as a mechanic.

On arrival in Egypt in mid-April, the squadron's mechanics were split up into several parties and assigned to British units for training. Bennett joined No. 14 Squadron, Royal Flying Corps, and trained as a fitter and turner. After returning to his own unit, he gained promotion to corporal on 24th August and later that year he began duty with No. 67 Squadron, R.F.C., an all-Australian squadron serving with the British Expeditionary Force in Egypt.

He remained with No. 67 Squadron throughout the Sinai and Palestine campaigns and was promoted to sergeant in March 1918. It was not long after his promotion that he was mentioned in dispatches, and awarded the Meritorious Service Medal for his distinguished service as an air mechanic.

After the war Bennett, along with Sergeant W. H. Shiers, was invited to join Captain Ross Smith as air mechanics. Ross was then attempting the first Cairo-Calcutta flight in a Handley-Page aircraft and both mechanics received the Air Force Medal for outstanding work under hazardous conditions during the flight. The same crew then carried out a survey by ship of the proposed Calcutta-Koepang (Timor) air route. On 7th July 1919 Bennett was attached to a Royal Air Force unit on the north-west frontier in India; here he superintended the rigging of Bristol fighters for use in reconnaissance and offensive missions during the short but fierce Afghan campaign.

After his success with Ross and the rest of the Vickers team in the Britain to Australia race, Bennett and Shiers both received Bars to their Air Force Medals but popular opinion at the time called for greater recognition for the mechanics, especially after Ross Smith stated publicly that the success of the flight was mainly due to their skill and zeal. So on 19th March 1920 the minister for defence announced that Bennett had been promoted senior warrant officer, class 1, and six months later he was granted the honorary rank of lieutenant in the A.I.F. reserve of officers.

Early in 1922 the Smith brothers decided to attempt a round-the-world flight and Bennett and Shiers were again chosen as mechanics. The crew planned to take off from England on 25th April, but on 13th April, Ross Smith and Bennett were killed during a test flight at Weybridge, when their Vickers Viking Amphibian crashed. The pioneer aviators were mourned as national heroes and their bodies were brought back to Australia. Bennett was buried in St Kilda cemetery on 19th June 1922 after a lying-in-state at Queen's Hall, Parliament House. An obelisk in his honour was unveiled at St Kilda on 26th April 1927.

## The Aircraft:

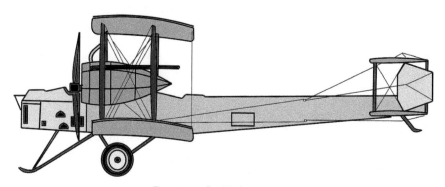

Drawing of a Vickers Vimy

The Vickers Vimy was a British heavy bomber developed and manufactured during the latter stages of the First World War by Vickers to equip the Royal Flying Corps.

The prototype (B9952) was conceived and designed by Vickers chief designer, Reginald Kirshaw Pierson and was first flown on the 30th November 1917.

Four prototypes were built and each was fitted with a different powerplant for testing, including engines manufactured by Salmson of France, Hispano Suisa of Spain, Sunbeam, Fiat and Rolls-Royce with the production modal FB27A using the Rolls-Royce Eagle V111 engine.

The production Vimy can best be described as an equal-span, twin-engine, four-bay biplane, with balanced ailerons on both upper and lower wings. The engine nacelles are positioned mid-gap and contained the fuel tanks. It had a biplane tail with elevators on both upper and lower surfaces and twin rudders. The main undercarriage consisted of two pairs of wheels supported on tubular steel V-struts. There was both a tail-skid and an additional skid mounted below the nose of the fuselage to prevent nose-overs.

The aircraft was designed to accommodate a three-man crew and a payload of 12 bombs. In addition to the pilot's cockpit, which was positioned just ahead of the wings, there were two positions for gunners, one behind the wings and the other in the nose, each with a pair of Scarff-ring mounted Lewis guns.

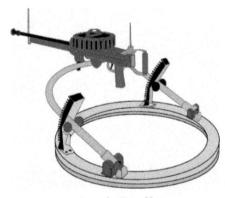

Drawing of a Scarff-ring

Provision for a maximum of four spare drums of ammunition were present in the nose position, while up to six drums could be carried in the rear position. The majority of the Vimy's payload of usually, twelve 250 lb bombs were stowed vertically inside the fuselage between the spars of the lower centre section. In some variants further bombs could be stowed externally for a total of 18 bombs, if the particular engine used provided enough power.

For attacks on surface shipping the Vimy could also be armed with two torpedoes. To improve bombing accuracy, the Vimy was equipped with the High-Altitude Drift Mk.1a bombsight. Standard equipment also included two Michelin built Mk.1 flare carriers.

The first FB27 was sent to Martlesham Heath for official trials in January 1918 where it was well received after demonstrating that it could lift a much heavier payload than its main competitor, the Handley Page 0/400 which boasted twice the power of the FB27.

Only a small number of aircraft had entered service by the time the armistice was signed on the 11th November 1918 so the Vimy never actually saw action during the war and although it had been ordered in large numbers, many of the contracts were subsequently cancelled. Nevertheless, the Vimy became the core of the RAF's heavy bomber force throughout the 1920s and a dedicated transport derivative of the Vimy, the Vickers Vernon, became the first troop transport aircraft operated by the RAF.

A Vickers Vernon in flight

The Vimy achieved success as both a military and civil aircraft, the latter using the Vimy's Commercial variant but the Vimy is probably best remembered for being the aircraft piloted by John Alcock and Arthur Brown on their epic, first non-stop crossing of the Atlantic Ocean in June 1919.

The Vimy continued to be operated until the 1930s in both military and civil capacities.

The Vimy Commercial was a civilian version of the aircraft with a larger-diameter fuselage made mostly from spruce plywood.

A Commercial Vimy on the ground

It was developed at Joyce Green airfield in Kent and first flown from there on 13th April 1919. Initially, it bore the interim civil registration *K-107*, later being re-registered as *G-EAAV*.

The prototype entered the 1920 race to Cape Town; it left Brooklands on 24th January 1920 but crashed at Tabora, Tanganyika on 27th February that same year.

Vickers built a total of 147 aircraft at Bexley Heath, Crayford and Weybridge and others were built under contract by Clayton & Shuttleworth Ltd. Kingsbury Aviation Co, Metropolitan Wagon Company, Morgan & Company, The Royal Aircraft Factory and Farnborough and Westland Aircraft Works.

**Commercial Vimy interior**

The aircraft supplied to Ross and his team was fitted with two Rolls-Royce Eagle Mark V111 engines, of which there were only four in existence, the other two having been fitted to the machine in which Alcock and Brown had crossed the Atlantic, and Claudel-Hobson carburettors. The aircraft's 720 h.p. gave it a maximum speed of 110 m.p.h. It had a landing speed of 45 m.p.h. and with a cruising speed of 90 m.p.h; fuel consumption was rated at 34 gallons per hour and oil at 1 gallon per hour. The fuel tanks had a capacity of 516 gallons. The aircraft was built in the Vickers factory at Weybridge-on-Thames with the propellers supplied by the Lang Propeller Company.

## The Flight

The Vickers Vimy team took off from Hounslow just after 9 a.m. on 12<sup>th</sup> November 1919 just five months after Alcock and Brown had successfully flown non-stop across the Atlantic Ocean in a similar aircraft.

The Vickers Vimy team in front of their aircraft

For some reason the Vickers company appeared at first to be reluctant to enter an aircraft in the race. It was only after General Borton, (who had wanted to enter the race himself but not being Australian was ineligible), kept insisting that they should provide a machine for Ross Smith, who had been with Borton on the survey from India to Australia and who had already flown a Handley Page from London to Palestine, that the company subsequently changed their mind and made the Vimy available.

Despite the company's early reluctance to enter an aircraft, once committed they did all they could to support Ross and his team in their endeavour, as did the Shell Company and

Wakefield Oil Ltd. who undertook to make the necessary fuel and oil available when needed along the route.

The Shell Company had in fact, always been willing to help aviation pioneers in any way they could with record breaking attempts. After all, it made for good advertising.

The team wanted to take as much as they could with them in the way of spares, so it was decided that only items of practical use would be taken on the flight. Ross had planned everything meticulously, and had decided that the all up weight of the air-

Advert for Shell Oil and Petrol

craft was not to exceed 13.000 lb, despite the fact that Alcock and Brown's had been 14,000 lb crossing the Atlantic. After spares and tools had been stowed away in every nook and cranny of the aircraft it had weighed 13,300 lb, and so apart from shaving gear, a tooth brush and the clothes they wore, all the crew's personal effects were transported separately by sea.

The Vimy crew put a great deal of emphasis on pre-flight preparation and forward planning. Not only did Bennett and Shiers overhaul and familiarise themselves with the Vimy's engines while Ross and Keith Smith studied and memorised countless landmarks to look out for en route, but all four of them undertook fitness training to ensure they were in the best physical condition they could be.

Two small luxuries that they took with them were some Bournville chocolate, and some Wrigley's chewing gum. The latter, when well chewed, was often used for running repairs, especially to fuel lines.

Registration markings had recently been introduced for international travel and those allocated to the Vimy were G-

EAOU. When asked what the letter stood for, the crew would answer, "God 'Elp All Of Us".

The first Armistice Day, the 11th November seemed a good symbolic day to start as the early morning fog had lifted and the rain had stopped. After a brief flurry of snow they took off from Weybridge, where the aircraft had been prepared, and flew to their starting point at Hounslow.

The next day, again after early fog, the Vimy was rolled out of its hangar and officials from the Royal Aero Club affixed the necessary seals that the race rules required.

Just before 9 a.m. they took delivery of a bag of mail and a copy of the London Times for Sir Ronald Munro Ferguson, the Australian Governor-General, along with messages of support from Prince Albert, that read, "*May good fortune attend you in your sporting attempt*," and from Major-General Seely, "*I wish you all good luck in your sporting flight.*"

Despite unfavourable weather reports Ross took the decision to take off at 9.05 a.m. An over enthusiastic press photographer, obviously anxious to get a dramatic picture of the take off, had positioned himself at the end of the runway. Wally Shiers later reported that visibility had been very bad and that they had felt a jolt just as they left the ground, which caused them some concern. Fortunately, the aircraft was undamaged, but the photographer's equipment was smashed beyond repair and he was lucky to escape the incident with his life.

Their great adventure did not start well, as when they left the white cliffs of Dover behind them and crossed the French coast, conditions worsened. They ran into cloud fronts that had to be avoided and visibility was almost zero, rendering them uncertain of their exact position. Heavy snow meant that they had to remove their goggles in the open cockpit and Ross later wrote in his diary, "*This sort of flying is a rotten game. The cold is hell, and I am silly for having ever embarked on the flight*".

After some six hours of awful weather the cloud thinned out and some sun broke through. Coffee from their flasks revived them a little although their sandwiches were frozen solid. The careful studying of their route and landmarks paid off and they realised that the town at the end of the valley below them was Roanne, only 40 miles from their destination of Lyons. When they landed at Lyons the French ground crew were amazed that they had flown from London in such bad weather, and Ross later said that the flight from London to Lyons in 6 hours and 20 minutes was the most difficult leg of the journey. The one heartening thing however, was the fact that their navigation had been spot on, even in the most appalling conditions.

After refuelling, (a task that was probably the most gruelling of all their regular chores, simple because it involved lifting dozens of four gallon cans some six feet up a ladder to Keith, who then emptied the cans into the Vimy's fuel tanks through a funnel that had been fitted with a chamois leather to act a filter, and pre-heating the water in the radiators) they took off from Lyons shortly after 10 a.m. the next morning, the 13th November.

Although frosty, the weather was far better than the previous day's, and good visibility meant that the French countryside was spread out before them all the way to Cannes and then Nice, where Ross flew low for the benefit of a large crowd that had assembled on the promenade.

Their intention had been to reach Rome that day, but the delays setting off, coupled with a strong headwind that confronted them after crossing the Italian boarder en route to San Remo, upset their plans. They were still almost two hours flying time from Rome and a night landing in the days before the introduction of landing lights was never a good idea, so the decision was made to land at Pisa instead.

An unscheduled landing at that time was no big deal, un-expected aircraft often turned up and were always made wel-come. Similarly, if an overseas aircraft failed to arrive when expected, it would not cause any great worry until at least a month passed.

On landing at Pisa they were happy to find an R.A.F. officer stationed there, who helped them find accommodation for the night while Shiers replaced a broken manifold.

It had been raining for some time and the aircraft had actu-ally skidded several yards on landing, but despite the rain con-tinuing overnight and virtually flooding the airfield, Ross and the crew were reluctant to endure another delay and made an attempt to take off the next morning. After taxiing only a few yards the Vimy became bogged down in mud and the efforts of as many as thirty ground crew failed to dig her out.

The next day, the 15$^{th}$ November, looked no better weath-erwise, but again determined to avoid further delay, Ross and Keith Smith searched the airfield for a solid strip of ground long enough for a take off. After choosing what looked like a suitable area the crew embarked, but as theVimy turned for take off, one wheel sank into a soft patch of mud. Bennett and Shiers, along with several Italian groundcrew managed to free the aircraft and line it up for take off.

Shiers took his place in the aircraft while Bennett, draped himself over the rear fuselage to stop the nose of the Vimy dipping when Ross applied the throttle. With groundcrew also assisting the initial forward movement of the aircraft, Ross opened the throttles up and with very little runway left, the Vimy was once again airborne. Bennetts instructions, if he was unable to scramble aboard at the last minute, were to catch the next train to Rome and re-join the team in the capital. As things worked out, Bennett was virtually dragged aboard the aircraft at the last minute by Shiers, and took his position in the aircraft unscathed by his hazardous embarkation.

About an hour after leaving Pisa, Ross noticed the oil-gauge for one of the engines was reading zero. Not knowing whether this was due to a lack of oil or a faulty gauge, he was left with no option other than to shut the engine down and search for a suitable landing place. In the end Ross managed to land the Vimy on one engine at Venturina, just inland from the Etruscan Coast of Tuscany, where Wally Shiers quickly identified and rectified the problem that turned out to be with the oil gauge.

After the problem was resolved the Vimy took off into a strong headwind that reduced their groundspeed considerably, so it must have been a great relief to finally touch down at Centocelle aerodrome, Rome, later that day.

There was always great comaraderie between aviators of all nationalities, so the British Air Attaché and members of the Italian Air Force made Ross and his team more than welcome and were full of both praise for their undertaking and helpful advice. The original intention on leaving Rome had been to fly non-stop to Athens but they were advised that it would be safer to fly first to Taranto, then on to Suda Bay and then Cairo.

Whilst in Rome the team received a cable from Prime Minister Hughes that read, *"Desire congratulate you and your party on your successful start and wish you every success on your great adventure. While the Government and people of Australia hope that an Australian aviator may be the first to fly from Europe to Australia and thus achieve what will easily be the world's record in aerial navigation, I urge you to take no unnecessary risks. Do your best but do nothing foolhardy. If you cannot make Australia in 30 days never mind. Good Luck."*

It is thought that in this message to Ross and his team, he referred to the flight being from Europe rather than Britain, because he was aware that at that time, Poulet had already arrived in India and was in the lead.

Deciding to take the advice they'd been given, they took off around 9 a.m. on the 16th November to fly to Taranto. Ahead of them lay the Apennine mountains, and low cloud forced them to pick a route through the valleys, which remained cloud free. At first their account states that the journey through the valleys was a pleasant one and the scenery quite stunning, but soon turbulence began tossing the flimsy machine around like a cork in a bottle, with Ross later reporting that at one point the aircraft dropped nearly a thousand feet. It was a great relief when they finally cleared the mountains and enjoyed a much smoother ride down the coast to Taranto.

Taranto had been an important port during the war and the British Army and Airforce still had a presence there. This enabled Ross to get an update on the condition of the runway at Suda Bay while Shiers and Bennett serviced the Vimy.

The runway at Suda Bay was reported as being in reasonable condition so the Vimy took off at 8.18 a.m. on the 17th November. Yet again the weather was less than ideal, forcing the team to divert slightly and follow the coast of Greece all the way down to Cape Matea. From there they flew over the islands of Kythera and Antikythera to the airfield at Suda Bay.

Although the R.A.F. Officer at the site wanted to show the crew around the picturesque locality, the crew were simply anxious to get to bed, with the following day's 650-mile flight to Cairo, at the forefront of their thoughts.

The leg of their journey from Crete to Cairo was almost entirely over water. As a precaution, in case the Rolls-Royce engines, which had been performing extremely well to date, decided that now was the time to play up, the crew inflated four innertubes to use as life-rafts if they came down in the sea.

After one last check of the engines, they took off at 8.12 a.m. on the 18th. Luckily, the cloud was just high enough to allow them to clear the mountain tops and Keith Smith plotted a direct course across the sea to Sollum. Although the flight over the sea was thankfully uneventful, the sight of the African coast when it came into view, must still have very welcome, and when the River Nile and the Pyramids were sighted the crew manage to relax and enjoy the view.

Both Ross and Wally Sheirs had been in Cairo during the war and were familiar with the surroundings, and putting off the usual maintenance jobs until the morning for once, the crew spent the evening on the terrace of the Shepherd's Hotel.

The original intention had been to spend a rest day in Cairo, but having lost time earlier and with the knowledge that Poulet was ahead of them by some 3,000 miles, they decided to push on. So the 19th November saw them take to the air again, bound for Damascus, Syria.

The flight from Cairo to Damascus took them over what was familiar ground, where they had served during the war. Who can say what memories would have been recalled, possibly a mixture of joyful camaraderie and sad loss. Ross, being so familiar with the land below them, would have found his way easily to the River Jordan and the Sea of Galilee, over which Keith would then have set course for Damascus.

Damascus was another of their destinations where they would have been welcomed by R.A.F. friends and colleagues and managed to get a good night's sleep after a decent meal in a good hotel.

The morning of the twentieth was one of heavy rain, the first seen in Damascus for over eight months, and the wheels of the Vimy were bogged down. Concerned that the rain would continue for several days and not wishing to fall even further behind Paulet in the Caudron, they decided to dig the Vimy out of the mud and press on.

Once again Ross's exceptional skill saved the day and in what must have been a chaotic whirlpool of flying mud from the propellers of the twin engines, the Vimy rose confidently into the air.

They now benefited from some decent weather that must have come as a welcome change but ironically, the only thing the good visibility enabled them to see was sand. Below them was a vast expanse of desert stretching all the way to their next landmark, Tadmur. From there they plotted a course to intercept the Euphrates River that they could then follow to where it comes close to the Tigris and Baghdad. They joined the Euphrates at Abu Kemal and turned South-East. Unfortunately, this had them flying directly into a strong headwind that seriously impeded their progress, and it soon became clear that they would be unable to make Baghdad in daylight.

Below them, still some forty miles from Baghdad, was the First World War battlefield of Ramadie, where an Indian Cavalry regiment was encamped. Fortunately, there was also a half decent landing strip, so the decision to land there was not a difficult one. On landing, Ross and his team were delighted to discover that a quantity of fuel was also kept at the base and that this would be enough to keep the Vimy in the air past Baghdad and on to Basra, a further 350 miles.

Good fortune, as so often seems the case, soon turned to bad as not long after their evening meal in the mess, gale force winds swept in and threatened to blow the aircraft over and cause serious, or even irreparable damage.

Quick and decisive action was required, but there was no shortage of willing help. As many as fifty Cavalry Officers and soldiers helped to hold the plane down as Ross climbed aboard, started the engines and managed to turn the Vimy head on into the wind. Throughout the night men fought to hold the plane down, even having to lie across the ailerons to prevent them flapping violently up and down as their cables broke.

In the morning, with the wind much reduced in ferocity, the damage to the aircraft was assessed and apart from a quantity of broken cables and the fact that sand had infiltrated every tiny space of the machine the Vimy had survived its ordeal pretty much intact. Ross later said that the men of the 10$^{th}$ Indian Lancers had undoubtedly saved the Vimy and fully deserved the praise of all.

It was well after mid-day before all the sand had been cleared from the plane and the cables repaired, but the day was bright, and despite being the latest of any of their departures, they were soon in the air and flying over Baghdad on their way to Basra, a flight that took them some three hours.

It was now the 21st November and they were still over two weeks behind Poulet in the Coudron. Despite this, Ross was impressed with the R.A.F. maintenance facilities at Basra and decided that it would be worth staying one whole day there so that Bennett and Shiers could give the engines a complete overhaul, rather than just clean the plugs and check the magnetos.

At 6.35a.m. on the morning of the 23$^{rd}$ November 1919, the Vickers Vimy that took off from Basra bound for Bandar Abbas, Persia, was arguably in as good a condition as when it had left Hounslow eleven days earlier, despite the hammering it had taken at Ramadie. The Vickers Vimy was indeed proving to be one of the most robust and reliable aircraft of its day.

The flight from Basra to Bandar Abbas was a non-stop leg of some 630 miles that took them approximately eight hours. Although a flight of that length would have been very tiring, they nevertheless arrived at their destination in good spirits and immediately set about refuelling, before having a meal and retiring for the night.

The next leg of their journey was to be the longest of the whole trip. Between Bandar Abbas and Karachi lay 730 miles of inhospitable terrain, inhabited by a variety of frequently violent, warring tribes, whose reaction to a forced landing by strangely clad men in an even stranger machine would be difficult to predict.

They took off at 7a.m. on the 24th November and followed the coast down the Gulf of Oman before turning inland towards Karachi, known later as the "gateway to India."

On landing, after a thankfully uneventful flight, a jubilant crew were informed by R.A.F. personnel stationed at Karachi, that Poulet and Benoist were reportedly still in Delhi, only one day ahead of them, extraordinary when one considers that the Caudron had left Paris 43 days earlier, whereas the Vimy had only been in transit for twelve. The fact that the Vimy was making so much better progress than the Caudron was probably down to two factors, firstly the amount of preparation and forward planning that Ross and his team had invested in the endeavour and secondly, the fact that the Vickers Vimy was a heavy bomber producing 750 h.p. compared to the 160 h.p. of the light reconnaissance Caudron.

The Vimy's flight to Delhi started a little before 8 a.m. on 25th November and the 9-hour flight was one of contrasting scenery. After passing Hyderabad there was a three-hour flight over the Sind Desert before the terrain changed to one of green fields and rivers after Ajmere.

On reaching Delhi, Ross decided that, despite the gruelling journey they had just completed, but always aware of the importance of good publicity, to make a circuit of the city in order to give the inhabitants a chance to see the Vimy in flight. Ross would also have noticed the absence of Poulet's Caudron as he made his approach to the aerodrome, and rightly surmised that he must have left that morning.

Even though Poulet had already left Delhi by the time the Vimy arrived, Ross was in no doubt that they would be able to overtake him in plenty of time to reach Darwin before him, so it was with this confidence that it was decided to spend the first part of the 26<sup>th</sup> November working on the aircraft and the second part sightseeing.

The next leg of their journey was to Calcutta, but as this was some 850 miles from Delhi, it was considered too great a distance to cover in one go, and so Allahabad had been selected as an intermediate stop.

About an hour into their fight, history decided to repeat itself when Ross was forced to make an unscheduled landing at Muttra, north west of Agra, the second forced landing of their trip, when the oil-gauge once again registered zero. On landing, Shiers quickly resolved the problem, which turned out to be exactly the same as when they had left Pisa, the indicator needle was slipping.

In the air again they were soon flying over the Taj Mahal, of which Keith took many photographs, en route to Allahabad.

Image of the Taj-Mahal taken by Keith Smith from the Vimy

Again there was no sight of Poulet's Caudron when they arrived at Allahabad, but there was a communication for them from Prime Minister Hughes, who was now anxious that they should arrive before Poulet.

It read, "Heartiest congratulations on your progress and best wishes for your safety and for a splendid victory."

Another early start at 8.30a.m. the next morning the 28th November, saw them en route to Calcutta, a destination that, apart from Keith, was familiar to the team, with it being the starting point for the survey they had carried out with Brigadier-General Borton aboard, first the Sphinx and then the Minto.

Although there was, of course, some interest in Britain in the events taking place with updates on the progress of competitors being reported in the Sunday Times, it was less than in some other parts of the world. A far-sighted Chinese government for example, had ordered 100 Vickers Vimy aircraft for their internal transport requirements after being impressed by its performance. India was also becoming very aviation minded, and the citizens of Calcutta were taking a keen interest in the race having just witnessed the arrival of Poulet the day before and his departure that morning.

The race-course was the designated landing site but in reality was too small, resulting in a tricky landing, but once again Ross, with all his experience and skill, was equal to the task. However, as they were coming to a halt the large crowd that had assembled to greet them, broke through the barriers that had been erected and it was with some difficulty that the police and army guards kept them from swamping the aircraft.

The plan had been to fly from Calcutta to Rangoon, but the 29th November was a Saturday, and because Saturdays were race days in Rangoon and the only suitable landing site was once again the race-course, this plan had to be altered, and so it was decided that they would land at Akyab instead.

The Vickers Vimy in Calcutta

Accepting a small amount of mail bound for Australia, the team took off at 8.30 a.m. The take off was not the easiest they had experienced due to a bird, probably one of the hawks for which Calcutta and the race-course in particular was renowned, flying into the propeller soon after they left the ground. The incident would have been disastrous had the propeller been damaged and caused the Vimy to crash. Fortunately, in this early example of bird-strike, the only casualty was the hawk. Nevertheless, Ross was acutely aware of the many birds circling the aircraft as they ascended, who were no doubt curious about the strange new visitor to their domain.

Their journey took them over the River Ganges to Chittagong, where the Sphinx had blown up, bringing back bad memories for three members of the crew.

After they passed Chittagong Ross followed the coastline to Akyab, and on arriving must have been elated to spot Poulet's Caudron on the ground. They had caught up with the Frenchman at last.

After landing safely, Ross taxied the Vimy to a spot next to the French aircraft, dwarfing the tiny Caudron.

As already mentioned, it is perhaps a measure of the man that, obviously disappointed to realise that he was now unlikely to archive his goal, Poulet pushed ahead of the crowd and was the first to greet Ross with outstretched hand and congratulate him on his achievement.

After a night exchanging stories of their adventures so far and congratulating each other on their achievements, Ross and Poulet agreed to depart together in the morning and travel with each other at least for a while. However, it would seem that the Vimy crew had, uncharacteristically, neglected some maintenance tasks that night, so although the Caudron took off at 6.30 a.m. the Vimy didn't manage to leave until 7.30 a.m. awarding Poulet and Benoist a good 60 mile lead.

When they did get away, they followed the coastline for a while before turning inland and flying over the Arakan mountain range to pick up the Irrawaddy River, which they followed as far as the town of Prome, after which they picked up the railway line leading to Rangoon on the south coast.

When they arrived at Rangoon, they must have expected a crowd to greet them but could not have imagined an estimated 40,000 would turn out, even though two aircraft were expected in one day and it would have, most likely, been the first aircraft any of them had seen.

It was almost mid-day when the team landed and were greeted by the Lieutenant-Governor Sir Reginald Craddock and his wife. There had been some concern among the team, having had no sighting of the Caudron on their journey, that Poulet had not arrived before them, but this turned to relief when the little Poulet made a good landing at 12.50 p.m. to a similar ovation as that received by Ross and his team.

Burmese troops mounted guard over the two aircraft as a large number of the crowd who had gathered to greet them had decided to celebrate by setting up camp and staging an impromptu festival.

Once again the two crews had decided to take off and journey together the next morning, this time because the next leg of the journey to Bangkok involved flying over some dense and mostly unexplored jungle. The rationale was that if one had to make a forced landing the other would be able to direct any recue party and save days of unnecessary searching.

Once again, just after daybreak, fate played its hand and interfered with their plans. Although the Vimy started up well, Poulet and Benoist were only able to get one of the Caudron's engines started. After waiting a while to see if Poulet could start the Caudron's second engine, it was with regret that Ross and his crew took off alone at 7 a.m. on the 1st December 1919 en route to Bangkok. The take-off was not an easy one. The racecourse was not long enough for the Vimy to get airborne with any margin of error and it did in fact clip the top of a tree after just clearing the boundary fence.

Poulet, who had watched the take-off, later reported that if the Vimy had been only a foot lower it would certainly have been damaged and may well have crashed.

Crossing the Gulf of Mataban they headed for the Thai border. Flying at a height of 4,000 feet to keep under some dense cloud, Ross knew that ahead of them lay the Tenasserim Hills, a range of mountains that boasted peaks of 7,000 feet. He was faced with a difficult choice. In order to get above the mountains he would have to gain at least another 3,000 feet, and that would put them flying over a mountain range in cloud with zero visibility. The alternative was to rely on charts, the

accuracy of which was uncertain, but which showed a pass
through the mountains.

Ross decided that keeping under the cloud base was the
least dangerous option and followed the pass through the
mountains. After about ten miles, the pass began to get increasingly narrow. Unsure how narrow it would become, and
not wanting to be boxed in and forced to ascend into cloud
Ross had no option but to turn back before it was too late. As
it was the Vimy only just managed to circle back with a clearance of only a few feet between wing tip and cliff face.

After consulting with his brother, who was navigating, the
decision was taken to try again, but this time to climb, hopefully, above the clouds. They emerged above the cloud at
9,000 feet, but circling again and once again travelling in the
right direction, they could see that the mountains ahead of
them rose even higher, and that they were still obscured by
cloud.

They nevertheless continued on course, taking the Vimy up
to its maximum operational altitude of 11,000 feet. Visibility
was poor, but at least at that altitude the mountains were below them.

Conditions for the crew at 11,000 feet in open cockpits
would have been very unpleasant, so Ross would have been
anxious to descend as soon as possible. However the maps and
charts of the area they were using had not been compiled with
aviation in mind. In view of this, Ross stayed at high altitude
until he could be confident they were past the mountains. Another reason for wishing to descend as soon as possible was to
get their bearings. Flying in cloud is difficult and it's easy to
become disorientated. Ross was aware that they may have de-
viated from course and he needed sight of the ground.

Descending cautiously, fearful that they might encounter
a mountain top at any moment, they held their breath, and

probably cheered as the Vimy finally imerged below the cloud into brilliant sunshine at 4,000 feet.

Sighting the Chao Phraya river Ross followed it into Bangkok and landed safely at Don Muang airfield where they were greeted by the British Consul Mr. T.H. Lyle.

During an inspection of the Vimy's two engines it was discovered that two valves needed to be reground, and as the airfield was home to the Thai Army Air Division it was equipped with all the necessary maintenance tools, Shiers and Bennett worked through the night to get the engines in best condition for the next leg of their journey.

The plan had been to fly all the way to Singapore, but on learning that there was a decent aerodrome at Singora, roughly half way, where there was fuel available, it was decided to stop there instead.

The journey between Rangoon and Bangkok typified the roller-coaster ride of emotions the crew must have gone through on their quest, one moment being cold, uncomfortable, flying blind and fearful of their endeavours ending in injury or death, and the next experiencing the friendly comradeship, admiration and hospitality of fellow aviators, ground crew and even politicians.

The next morning must have been a highlight for the four airmen, as they left Bangkok in good weather with an escort of four Thai Aviation Corps Nieuport and Brequet aircraft, which flew with them for the first fifty miles before dipping their wings in salute and turning back.

The good weather that had witnessed their departure from Bangkok soon changed to that of cloud and heavy rainfall. In order to navigate it was necessary to view the ground, but this was next to impossible while wearing goggles in heavy rain in an open cockpit, so goggles had to be removed. However, the rain was so heavy that it was painful to keep their eyes open for long without shielding them. For this reason, the two brothers took it in turns to keep watch. Thankfully the weather improved as they approached the airfield at Singora, but their troubles were by no means over.

The sight that confronted them showed that although the concept of powered flight was no longer new to people in 1919, many had no idea what was involved and just what an aircraft required in order to land and take off. It was obvious that somebody had been instructed to clear away the trees and create a landing site for aircraft, but that somebody had apparently no idea just how an aircraft landed. The trees had been cut down all right, but they had left the stumps sticking out of the ground, some by as much as 18 inches, more than enough to completely destroy the undercarriage of any aircraft.

Ross circled the airfield several times before selecting a route into a landing strip which, although it meant landing with a crosswind, looked the least hazardous. It took every ounce of skill he had to land the Vimy in one piece, the only damage being a broken tail skid. However when the crew walked back over the route, following the wheel tracks the aircraft had left, it was obvious that good fortune had also played a role in their safe landing, and that several tree stumps had been missed by no more than inches.

Their disappointment at the state of the landing ground and the damage sustained to the tail-skid was only compounded on the discovery that the supply of fuel was not only far less than expected, but had been ordered by Poulet and was destined for his Coudron, not the Vimy. But once again Ross showed that he was not a man to be thwarted by circumstance. He sent a telegram to the Shell agent at the Asiatic Petroleum Company in Penang requesting that 200 gallons of petrol be sent straight away, and another to the British Commissioner asking if he could assist in any way with the dispatch of the fuel. Ross also sent a request to the Governor of

Singora, asking for a number of tree-stumps to be removed in order to clear a runway for their take-off.

Whilst Ross busied himself with organising fuel and runways, Jim Bennett went in search of materials to mend the skid, and on locating the necessary steel, he had the repair completed before 11 p.m. that evening. Accommodation for the night was supplied by H.R.H. Prince Yugala in the form of a comfortable and well-appointed bungalow. Just after Bennett had completed the repairs to the aircraft and was looking forward to a night's sleep, the rain that had been falling steadily was joined by gale force winds.

Fearful for the safety of the aircraft despite the fact that they had tied it down, all four airmen rushed to the airfield to find the Vimy being buffeted dangerously by the wind. They were forced to spend the night in vigil at the aircraft's side, physically holding it down when the winds were at their strongest. Daybreak saw the winds abate, and four wet, weary airmen struggled back to the bungalow in search of breakfast, but most importantly, the Vimy was safe.

During the day a large workforce of Malay volunteers had prepared a 50 yards wide runway of sufficient length, and all that was needed for the Vimy to take to the air was the arrival of the fuel from Penang.

The fuel arrived later in the day but, as it was still raining and refuelling involved lifting 50 heavy drums of petrol up to the fuel tanks, it was considered prudent to refuel in the morning.

The 4th December 1919 was Ross Smith's twenty-seventh birthday but there was no time to celebrate if they wanted to be airborne and on their way to Singapore by 10.15.a.m.

Although the ground at the airfield wasn't boggy at all, the heavy rains had deposited a layer of water several inches deep on much of the site. After inspecting the ground Ross decided that the water would not interfere enough to prevent the Vimy gaining the necessary speed for take-off.

At one point, after encountering a couple of large puddles the Vimy's speed dropped considerably and Ross was faced with either aborting the take-off or chancing that they would pick up sufficient speed again before the airstrip came to an end. He chose the latter, and in the end was able to clear the end fence, but only by the narrowest of margins.

Singapore racecourse was a checkpoint arranged by the Royal Aero Club that all the competitors had to visit, but it was not very big and posed a problem for the Vimy when landing. In these days of "health and safety" the plan to land the aircraft in such a short distance, referred to as "operation slow down," sounds foolhardy in the extreme. It had been agreed that as soon as the wheels of the Vimy touched the ground, Jim Bennett would climb out of his cockpit and slide down the top of the fuselage to the tailplane, thus positioning his weight on top of, or as near as possible to the tail skid, bringing the aircraft to a stop much quicker. When Ross was on final approach, he cut the engines, gliding the Vimy in at as slow an airspeed as he considered safe. As agreed, just before the wheels touched the ground, Bennett climbed out of his cockpit, and watched anxiously by Wally Shiers, who was willing him not to lose his balance, clambered down the fuselage. Fortunately for all concerned their plan worked and the Vimy came to a halt just one hundred yards from where the wheels first touched.

Having left Hounslow on the 12th November they now had seven days left in order to complete the race within the 30 days stipulated in the rules. Ross had four more stops planned before crossing the Australian coast, so it was decided to spend the next day working on the aircraft to ensure it was in the best possible condition for the remaining 2,500 miles to Darwin.

Working on the Vimy at Singapore

The main problem facing Ross was getting the Vimy back into the air from such a short runway. In the end, having taken on more fuel, it was decided to lighten the load as much as possible by leaving some equipment behind. Having already restricted what they could take with them on previous occasions, this time it was some of the photographic equipment that was left behind.

So, early on the morning of the 6th December, the Vimy and its intrepid crew took off for Indonesia. They had made sure that no part of the landing strip would be wasted by manoeuvring the tail of the aircraft up against the fence at the far end of the racecourse, ensuring that they could make use of the full length available. They were almost out of runway when Ross eventually pulled back on the stick and once again, they made it into the air by the skin of their teeth.

Before heading off for Sumatra, Ross made a circuit around Singapore for a last look at the city, and it wasn't long before they found themselves flying through alternating rain and then sunshine and turbulence.

After crossing the equator the Vimy passed over the island of Muntok, now Bangka, off the east coast of Sumatra, and the crew later said that this area was the most beautiful they had flow over. Dutch officials on the island notified Batavia, now Jakarta, by radio, and the position of the Vimy and its crew was radioed around the world. Nine hours after leaving Singapore they landed at Kalidjati, the headquarters of the Dutch Air Corps in that part of the world, and according to Ross, nestling at the foot of the mountains, the best aerodrome he had ever seen.

Four Glenn Martin aircraft, had been sent to meet the Vimy and escort it in but they somehow missed it and landed not long after its arrival. To greet Ross and his crew were officers of the Dutch Air Force as well as Count van Limburg Stirum, the Governor-General of the Netherlands Indies.

Ross and the Count had met before during the survey earlier in the year and the two men got on well. Both men were convinced that the islands were the natural place to construct aerodromes that would be needed for any commercial air service between Europe and Australia and had discussed the matter at length.

Before leaving England, Ross had cabled the Count, anxious to know if an aerodrome had been constructed at Bima and was now delighted to hear that not only was one being prepared at Bima, but also another one at Atamboea on the island of Timor.

The 7th of December saw them take off at 7.30 a.m. heading for Sourabaya just 350 miles distant. After an uneventful flight Ross circled the aerodrome before landing, as he had been unable to get a reliable report and wanted to assess its condition. The airfield, although shorter than Ross would have liked, at least appeared firm. Because of the lack of length of runway, Ross had planned to open up one engine and swing the machine round if it looked like overshooting, but in the end the planned manoeuvre proved unnecessary.

After a good landing the port wheels began to sink into the mud and the aircraft tilted forward onto its nose-skid, where-upon Ross shut down both engines and the Vimy settled back into her normal position.

It turned out that the aerodrome had been built on land re-claimed from the sea and after thousands of people turned up to greet the arrivals it had quickly turned into a muddy swamp.

After several ideas had been exchanged between officials and crew as to how to move the aircraft onto firmer land, bam-boo matting was laid down, and after several appeals for more of the same they eventually had enough to move the Vimy onto firm ground, although two punctures had to be repaired that had been caused by nails in the matting.

The Vimy at Sourabaya 7th December 1919

Although the Vimy was no longer bogged down, the problem still remained of just how they were going to take-off. Nothing that they had experienced up to then had seemed so much out of their control. It seemed that that their journey was at an end. Hindsight is a wonderful thing and if, instead of landing at Sourabaya, they had opted to fly the extra 420 miles to the new aerodrome at Bimba, the situation they found themselves in would have been avoided.

It was Keith Smith who suggested, maybe out of pure desperation, that if they could obtain enough bamboo matting to lay a double path the full length needed for take-off, they might still have a chance. Ross immediately put the idea to the Dutch official, and they promised to canvass the entire district for the necessary matting. If the crew were at all sceptical about their chances, their doubts were put to rest in the morning by the sight of Indonesians approaching from all directions laden down with matting. The fact that they may not get back what may well have been their only floor covering, meant nothing beside the fact the Australians needed help.

Matting continued to arrive throughout the morning and at one time there were as many as 200 people sorting, laying, and lacing mats together. So on the 8$^{th}$ December, it was not the usual skill and ingenuity of Ross and his crew that saved the Vimy from failure, it was the local population of Indonesians.

The bamboo matting runway

The first attempt to take-off failed when the bamboo matting was blown around by the slipstream. After pegging the matting down however, their second attempt to take-off from what they named the bamboo road was more successful and they were on their way to Bima, but not before circling the town to show their appreciation for the help they had been given.

The flight to Bima was unremarkable except for the fact that they noticed small splashes on the surface of the water, that they soon discovered were flying fish and they were amazed that they had been able to see them from a height of 3,000 feet.

The aerodrome at Bima had been clearly marked with a large white cross at its centre so Ross was able to spot it from several miles distant.

The local Sultan and the Dutch Commissioner met them on landing and offered the hospitality of a native bungalow a couple of miles from the landing strip, which they accepted. During the night they were disturbed on a couple of occasions by curious locals prowling about, but nevertheless managed to get some sleep. In the morning a large crowd had collected to see them off and gave them presents of cocoanuts.

Crowds gathered at Bima

After followng the north coast of Flore to Reo, one of the lesser Sunda Islands, they crossed to the south side of the island, where they spotted an active volcano in the distance, and were briefly tempted to fly over it and gaze into the smoking crater. The weather looked to be deteriorating however so instead they flew as far as Pandar before setting a course for Timor.

They landed safely at Atamboea on Timor, their last planned landing before Port Darwin.

The date was 9th December and it now seemed that nothing could stop them. Poulet was out of the running, having abandoned the flight at Moulmein, Wilkins had crashed at Suba Bay in Crete, Matthews was still in Vienna, Howell had crashed at Corfu and Parer had not yet left London.

The aerodrome at Atamboea was one of those specially made for the Australia flight by the Governor-General of the Netherlands Indies. It had been completed only the day before their arrival, but Dutch officials had thoughtfully arranged for petrol and oil supplies to be close by, saving them time and enabling them to carry out a thorough overhaul.

The crew's accommodation for the night was some six miles from the airfield, but a guard of Dutch soldiers kept watch over the Vimy throughout the night. Excitement prevented any of the team from getting much sleep that night and they were up before daybreak, only to be disappointed by the fact that thick haze was obscuring everything and delaying their departure until it lifted around 8.35 a.m.

On a lighter note, Ross reported later that a group of locals were sitting on a fence, being cooled by the slipstream from the propellers which were just ticking over, but as he opened up both engines for take-off, the sudden blast of air nocked them all backwards into the crowed behind, causing a great deal of both confusion and mirth.

Ross had been concerned that, as this was to be their longest flight over water, they would be out of sight of land for some five hours. Because of this concern, they secured a parcel of food and water, along with a Very pistol and some cartridges to the tail of the Vimy, remembering that when an aircraft lands in the sea, it will float for a while before the front sinks and only the tail remains above water.

The Australian Government had arranged for a warship, HMAS Sydney to be on patrol between Timor and Darwin in case the Vimy was to get into difficulty over water and it must have been a welcome sight at 11.48, when Keith spotted a smoke plume in the distance that did in fact turn out to be HMAS Sydney.

Ross could not resist sweeping low over the vessel so they could take a picture of the upturned faces and waving hands of the sailors.

Two hours after flying over the HMAS Sydney at 2.06 p.m. they sighted Bathurst Island Lighthouse and at 3.0 p.m. on 10th December 1919, after circling Darwin, they landed on Australian soil, 27 days and 20 hours after leaving Hounslow, thus winning the £10,000 prize with just 52 hours to spare.

A huge crowd had assembled to greet them and the formalities of passing through customs, and an official greeting by the Mayor of Darwin and the Administrator of the Northern Territory, were cut short when the team were hoisted shoulder high by the excited crowd and conveyed to the garden of the jail where howls of "Speech! Speech" rang out.

When the excitement of the crowd had abated somewhat the team where able to return to their aircraft, and make sure it was lashed down for the night.

Ross and the team had developed a great admiration for the machine and for those who had designed and built it. Ross later paid tribute to them, saying that the success of the venture was in great part due to them, and that they surely merited a large proportion of the praise. Not once since leaving Hounslow had she been under shelter, and yet Ross said that he could find neither fault nor flaw in her construction, and that given a few days overhaul on the engines, the Vimy would be quite capable of turning round and flying back to England.

The winning team had been unaware of the amount of world-wide interest there had been in the race, but now received a large number of congratulatery telegrams, one of which was from Prime Minister Hughes that read, *"In the name of the Commonwealth I greet you and your gallant companions on your safe arrival and I most heartily congratulate you on your magnificent achievement. You have covered the name of Australia with fresh laurels. You have broken all world's records and you have shown the world once more what manner of man the Australian is. You have given your country a world-wide advertisement and you have proved that with relays of machines and men Europe can be brought within 12 or 15 days of Australia."*

Before Ross had a chance to reply it was followed by another from Hughes, *"I sincerely trust you will give the Government the first opportunity of acquiring your machine for the Australian War Museum. It would be a lasting memorial of a great achievement."*

Celebrations continued at a formal dinner attended by The Royal Commissioner Mr Justice Ewing, after which the crew retired for the night at Government House.

For the next two days Ross answered messages of congratulations, still taken aback by the interest their flight had generated worldwide. It was in answering one of these that Ross asked if, as they were carrying some mail, a special stamp could be arranged. The Prime minister arranged for this to be done, although there was some misunderstanding as to whether it was to be a postage stamp or simply a date stamp.

At the time, a Universal Postal Union rule prohibited the use of commemorative stamps of "limited postal validity" in the international mail system. It was apparently on this basis that the Postmaster-General's Department refused to issue such a stamp. The solution was a stamp sized label that was not actually a postage stamp, so essentially a stamp design, but without a denomination. This was designed by Lieutenant George Benson (1887–1960), an official war artist at Gallipoli and the Western Front. As can be seen his design featured the Vickers Vimy aircraft flying over an Olympic torch, and maps of Great Britain and Australia, on a blue background.

The mail carried by Ross was received in Melbourne on 26 February 1920. A label was affixed to each cover, and a date stamp was applied to both the envelope and the label.

There were 576 labels printed by lithography from a copper block. Of the 576, at least 364 were affixed to the airmail covers, this number being those recorded in official government documents. Of the remainder, 125 stamps were held in reserve at the Note Printing Branch. These were destroyed on 6th September 1921, leaving 87 stamps to be accounted for. It is recorded that about 20 of these had the selvedge removed in readiness for affixing to covers, but they were not needed.

Several unused examples were presented at the time to the four airman and various officials, but otherwise the labels were held in a government department for several years. The printing block of the Ross Smith label was destroyed by government officials in 1948.

Commemorative stamp

Even though the race was over, they still had some 3,000 miles to travel to reach their home at Adelaide. Normally they would give the engines a complete overhaul before doing so, but the rainy season had just started and it seemed likely that they would have to delay for three months unless they started at once.

Four days after Ross and the team left Hounslow, Captain H.N. Wrigley and Sergeant A.W. Murphy had taken off from Melbourne in a BE2E in order to perform the first flight across the continent of Australia, and on the 12$^{th}$ December, as Ross and the team were servicing the Vimy ready to depart the next day, Captain Wrigley and Sergeant Murphy landed and taxied to a halt beside them. Both crews spent some time talking together and exchanging mutual congratulations on their achievements.

The next day at 10.23 a.m. the Vimy departed Port Darwin, and after following the telegraph line that joined Darwin and Adelaide for a few hours the starboard engine developed valve trouble, forcing them to land on a dried-up swamp. After landing safely Shiers quickly had the problem fixed, but as flying conditions were bad, they decided lay up until the morning and took shelter from the sun under the aircraft's wings.

The night however, was not a comfortable one, as they were attacked by mosquitos all night. They tried hiding under blankets, lighting fires and even covering themselves with whisky, which the mosquitos enjoyed a great deal, and because they didn't manage to get to sleep until the early hours, the departure in the morning was delayed until 10 a.m.

They followed the telegraph line as far as Newcastle Waters and then turned southwest (following directions they had been given by stockmen in Port Darwin) to follow the tracks of the cattle.

After an hour flying southwest they were horrified to hear a loud crack from the port propeller and see it split from boss to tip. Ross had spotted a tent pitch beside the cattle track up ahead of them so he shut off both engines and glided down to land close by. Thinking that they were now marooned some twenty miles from Anthony's Lagoon where there was a small police station and petrol depot, and dreading the thought that they would have to walk there, they were both astonished, and I'm sure delighted, to see two cars approaching.

Fortuitous timing had meant that a Mr Sydney Peacock and his son, who had been sinking a sub-artesian bore, was returning with Sergeant Stretton of the Mounted Police to strike camp and collect his tent. Had Ross and the team arrived an hour later, Mr Peacock and his tent would have been long gone.

After striking camp and leaving some much needed food and water for the aviators, Mr Peacock said he would arrange to have supplies sent out to them from Anthony's lagoon. He also left them a sheet of galvanised iron, which Bennett said he could use to repair the Vimy's propeller.

After three and a half days Bennett had completed what Ross later described as a unique and skilful repair to the propeller. Using pieces of a packing case to fill gaps, he glued the split portions together, bound them with strips of the galvanised iron, screwed in place with screw taken from the floor boards in the machine, and then the whole blade was covered in fabric and painted. In order to reduce any vibration caused by the increased weight, the opposite propeller had to be treated in the same manner. Bennett had carried out the repair so well that when the engines were started, there was, according to Ross, "*practically no vibration at all.*"

When they reached Charleville in Central Australia, the engines were given a complete overhaul and the damaged propeller was replaced, delaying their departure until 12th February 1920. Although the cost of the repairs and the new propeller were £459 . 16 . 5, no bill was ever sent to the Vimy crew and no request for payment ever made.

The wonderful reception that they had received in Darwin was nothing compared to what awaited them in Sydney where they flew over the harbour and the rooftops at 600 feet above the cheering crowds.

Even that however was surpassed on their final arrival in Melbourne where they were presented with the cheque for £10,000 by, the Prime Minister, the Right Hon. W.M. Hughes on behalf of the Commonwealth Government. It was also in Melbourne that Ross formally handed the Vickers Vimy over to the Commonwealth Government on behalf of Vickers Ltd. before flying it to Adelaide.

The authorities had planned a huge reception at the Flemington race-course in Melbourne and special trains had been laid on to carry spectators to the course to greet the airmen on the 24th February, but engine trouble delayed them until the next day.

The spectators waiting at Flemington race-course had contributed £1,680 after expenses that was to be given to worthy causes, and in the end it was decided to donate to other other airmen and their relatives who were in some way connected to the race. This proved a popular decision and the money was divided as shown.

| | |
|---|---|
| Mrs. Alice Douglas | £250 |
| Mrs. Elizabeth Ross | £250 |
| Relatives of Howell | £300 |
| Relatives of Fraser | £300 |
| Captain Wrigley | £50 |

| | |
|---|---|
| Warrent Officer Murphy | £50 |
| Each member of the Kangaroo team | £50 |
| Captain Matthews | £100 |
| Sergeant Kay | £100 |
| Lieutenant Parer | £100 |
| Lieutenant McIntosh | £100 |

Throughout the journey Keith Smith had taken a huge quantity of excellent photographs of both the Vimy and its crew as well as the extremely varied landscapes and weather conditions encountered. Those photographs won them first prize in the competition that Kodak had announced on the 30th May 1919, £1,000 in prize money for the best fifty negatives taken over the course of the race. The money was to be divided, £800 as a first prize, £150 for second, and £50 for third, and the firm had given each team fifty rolls of film to be used at the discretion of the cameraman.

Both Ross and Keith were knighted for their achievement; Sergeants W. H. Shiers and J. M. Bennett, were commissioned and awarded Bars to their Air Force Medals, and the £10,000 prize money was divided into four equal shares.

There had quite naturally been a great deal of speculation as to just what honours would be bestowed on the winning crew by King George V. When it was officially anounced that

Knighthoods of the Order of the British Empire were to be given to Ross and Keith Smith, but only Bars to their existing Air Force Medals for Sergeants Bennett and Shiers, it gave rise to some controversy. Many felt that it was grossly unfair, especialy as Ross Smith had declared in a speech made in Darwin, that their success was mainly due to Sergeants Bennett and Shiers, who had worked tremendously hard.

Questions were asked in the House of Representatives, with a Major Kerby stating that he for one would like to see more recognition for the two Sergeants, and suggested that they could recieve honorary commissions.

It turned out that in fact, although it was never announced in Parliament, Prime Minister Hughes had indicated that commissions be granted to both mechanics. On the 19th March 1920, the Minister for Defence announced that Segeant J. M. Bennett had been promoted to Officer Class1. and that Acting Sergeant W. A. Shiers was promoted to Sergeant, both appointments effective from the day they landed in Australia. Later, on the 1st September both Bennett and Sheirs were granted the honorary ranks of Lieutenants in the A.I.F.

Ross being presented with the £10,000 first prize

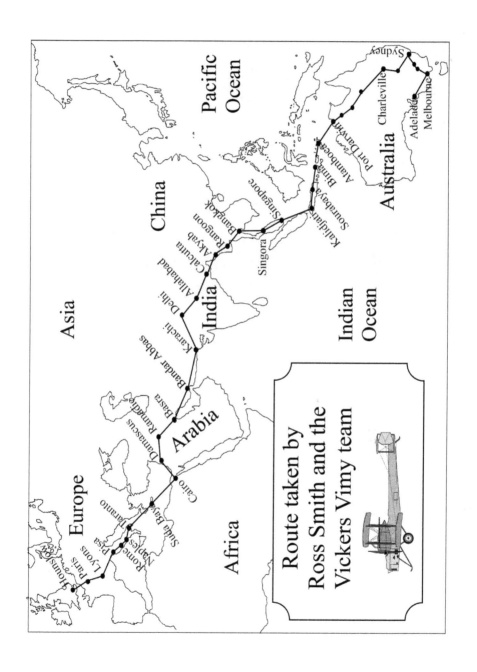

Route taken by
Ross Smith and the
Vickers Vimy team

ERECTED BY
THE COMMONWEALTH OF AUSTRALIA
TO COMMEMORATE THE LANDING
AT PORT DARWIN OF THE
FIRST AERIAL FLIGHT FROM ENGLAND
10TH DECEMBER 1919

**Monument at Port Darwin**

# Chapter 10

# What Next

The period leading up to the events detailed in this book and the inter-war years after, saw huge advances in aircraft and aero-engine design. The mono-plane took over from the bi-plane, and greater understanding of aerodynamics enabled faster than sound travel to become a reality. The timeline for many of those advances is shown here, together with other significant events of the time to relate them to.

### Events of 1919

1919 - First international commercial passenger air service initiated between Paris and Brussels.

March 3rd, 1919 - William E. Boeing, with Edward Hubbard as passenger, carries the first air mail from Canada to the U.S.

May 3rd, 1919 - The first Municipal Airport in the U.S. is dedicated at Atlantic City, New Jersey.

June 14th-15th, 1919 - Vickers Vimy: First nonstop flight across the Atlantic Ocean by British Capt. John Alcock and Lt. Albert Brown, from Newfoundland to Ireland.

December 10th, 1919 - Vickers Vimy G-EAOU lands in Darwin in Northern Australia thus completing the 135-hour journey from England to Australia.

## Events of the twenties
Pullman airliner shown at Olympia, 1920
First test sinking of a battleship by aerial bombardment, 1921
First flights of Bristol Bulldog 1927
First flight Dornier Do X flying boat 1929

## Events of the Thirties
1931 Empire State Building opens in US.
1932 First female solo transatlantic flight (Amelia Earhart)
Franklin Roosevelt elected president of US.
Frank Whittle's patent for jet engine finally granted, after being submitted in 1930.
1933 A Westland Wapitis, flown by Flt Lt David F. McIntyre   and powered by a Pegasus engine is the first aeroplane to fly over Mt. Everest.
First solo flight around the world.
US Prohibition ends
1936 First helicopter flight of over an hour
1937 Hindenburg disaster shatters public confidence in airships.
1938 First flight of pressurised transport aeroplane.
Germany occupies Austria
1939 World War Two begins
BOAC formed.

## Events of the Forties
1940 Evacuation of Dunkirk
Battle of Britain
1942 First jet combat aeroplane

1945 VE day. Atomic bomb dropped
1946 Pan-Am starts scheduled New York – London service
1947 International Civil Aviation Organisation established
Sound barrier broken (Chuck Yeager in the Bell X-1)
1948 Berlin airlift
1949 NATO formed


In 1934, The MacRobertson Trophy Air Race (also known as the London to Melbourne Air Race) took place in October as part of the Melbourne Centenary celebrations. The race was conceived by the Lord Mayor of Melbourne, Sir Harold Gengoult Smith, and the £15,000 prize money of was offered by Sir Macpherson Robertson, a wealthy Australian confectionery manufacturer, on the conditions that the race be named after his company. He also insisted that it was structured to be as safe as possible.

The race was once again organised by the Royal Aero Club. The starting point was RAF Mildenhall in East Anglia and it finished at the Flemington Racecourse, Melbourne, approximately 11,300 miles (18,200 km). Competitors could choose their own routes as long as they included the five compulsory stops, at Baghdad, Allahabad, Singapore, Darwin, and Charleville, Queensland. A further 22 optional stops were provided with stocks of fuel and oil provided by Shell and Stanavo. The Royal Aero Club put some effort into persuading the countries along the route to improve the facilities at the stopping points.

Although there was no limit to the size or power of aircraft used, and no limit to crew size, no pilot was allowed to join an aircraft after it left England. Aircraft had to carry three days' rations per crew member, floats, smoke signals, and efficient instruments.

There were prizes for the outright fastest aircraft, and for the best performance on a handicap formula by any aircraft finishing within 16 days.

The race was scheduled to start at dawn (6:30) on 20th October 1934. By then, the initial entrants that numbered over 60 had been whittled down to just 20, including three purpose-built de Havilland DH.88 Comet racers, two of the new generation of American all-metal airliners, and a mixture of earlier racers, light transports, and old bombers.

First off the line, watched by a crowd of 60,000, were Jim and Amy Mollison in the Comet "Black Magic", and they were early leaders in the race until forced to retire at Allahabad with engine trouble.

Jim and Amy Mollison (nee Amy Johnson)

The Mollison's de Havilland Comet 88, "Black Magic" lined up at Mildenhall

This left the DH.88 (Grosvenor House), flown by Flight Lt. C. W. A. Scott and Captain Tom Campbell Black, well ahead of the field, and they went on to win in a time of less than 3 days, despite flying the last stage with one engine throttled back because of an oil-pressure indicator giving a faulty low reading. They would have won the handicap prize as well, but the race rules stipulated that no aircraft could win more than one prize.

Significantly, both second and third places were taken by airliners, the KLM Douglas DC-2 PH-AJU Uiver ("Stork") and Roscoe Turner's Boeing 247-D. Both completed the course in less than a day more than the winner; KLM's DC-2 was even flying a regular route with passengers.

"Grosvenor House" G-ACSS, in Martin Place, Sydney 12 November 1934.

For me, the two things that highlight the advances in aviation between the 1919 air race from Britain to Australia and the 1934 MacRobertson Trophy Air Race are the overall design of the aircraft that took part. Even if you asked someone unfamiliar with the history of aviation, they could easily pick out which aircraft took part in which race.

The second and possibly more significantly, both second and third places were taken by airliners, the KLM Douglas DC-2 PH-AJU Uiver ("Stork") and Roscoe Turner's Boeing 247-D. Both completed the course in less than a day more than the winner.

KLM Douglas DC-2 PH-AJU Uiver ("Stork")

A Boeing 247-D. in flight

During the race, the Uiver, low on fuel after the crew had become lost when caught in a thunderstorm, ended up over Albury, New South Wales. Lyle Ferris, the chief electrical engineer of the post office at the time, went to the power station and signalled "A-L-B-U-R-Y" to the aircraft in Morse code by turning the town street lights on and off. Arthur Newnham, the announcer on radio station 2CO Corowa appealed for cars to line up on the racecourse to light up a makeshift runway. The Uiver landed successfully, and next morning was pulled out of the mud by locals to fly on to Melbourne and win the handicap section of the race, coming second overall.

Later that year the DC-2, on a flight from The Netherlands to Batavia, crashed (near Ar Rutba, Iraq), killing all seven on board; it is commemorated by a flying replica.

The whereabouts of the Trophy awarded to the winners went missing but after many years of speculation as to its whereabouts, it would now seem that an article in The Sydney Morning Herald, dated 24 January 1941, correctly stated that the trophy had been donated to the Red Cross to be melted down for the war effort.

As international civil aviation became increasingly affordable and civil airliners carried ever increasing numbers of passengers, air safety became much more of a concern. As aircraft developed and flew faster and higher, previously unforeseen problems came to light; problems such as metal fatigue, and the hazards of flying for long periods in freezing temperatures at high altitude.

Whereas, in the early days of civil aviation, a fatal air crash might involve a dozen or more lives, now hundreds could be killed in a single incident and lessons needed to be learned. The cause of every crash was vigorously investigated, and changes were made to both procedures and future designs based on the findings. Research and innovation went into, not only making civil aircraft less likley to crash, but also into making crashes more survivable if they occurred.

It is thanks to that level of study and commitment, that flying from Britain to Australia today is less hazardous that cycling from your home to the local supermarket.

What the rest of the twenty-first century will see as far as aviation is concered is as intriging as it is unpredictable, but an electric powered airoplane is certain to feature, as is sub-orbital passengers aircraft.

In June 2018 a Boeing 787 flew the route from Perth to London in 16 hours and 29 minutes.

Previously, all Australia-UK flights had stopped at least once en route to refuel, but improved technology and fuel efficiency means the 787 can cover the ground between Perth and London with a full payload without the need to stop.

Boeing 787-9 Dreamliner

Other books by Colin Holcombe

The Story of Flight ISBN: 978-1675480601 paperback

The Story of Flight ISBN: 978-1-71676-921-4
Extended edition (includes theory)

The Theory of Flight
For the Layman ISBN: 978-1-52727-290-3

Samuel Colt
The Man Behind the GunISBN: 978-1-78723-403-1